Couple Therapy

The Ultimate Guide to Build Healthy Relationships. Learn Practical Strategies to Improve Communication in Love Using the Self-Help Workbook. Overcome Conflicts, Jealously and Insecurity

Isabella Gray

Respective authors own all copyrights not held by the publisher.

The information herein is offered for informational purposes solely, and is universal as so. The presentation of the information is without contract or any type of guarantee assurance.

The trademarks that are used are without any consent, and the publication of the trademark is without permission or backing by the trademark owner. All trademarks and brands within this book are for clarifying purposes only and are the owned by the owners themselves, not affiliated with this document.

Table of contents:

Introduction

One of the most valuable qualities that you will acquire in life is communication, conversing with other persons. We interact with other people. It's straightforward occasionally, but it may feel impossible at other moments. This book will provide you with the skills to become a communicator who is more intuitive and efficient. Talking to someone you already meet will make you happier to figure out what keeps you from communicating with people you don't. During the process, you will communicate more openly and more often, and the contact will be sharper; most importantly, you will have a greater chance of achieving the answers you are hoping for. The individual you speak to wants to know as you understand them, and they still need to understand you, of course. True changes can be made, and relationships can flourish only until you enter a position of shared understanding. Two key types of connectivity occur. Primary communication-the exact terms that you utter and the clear sense that such terms provide to others. Secondary communication-when individuals presume or deduce from what you mean what you did not plan. Secondary contact exists beyond the actual words you say-from the perception you generate to the different meanings through which your phrases are available. Let's presume you're asking somebody you're paying a buddy to go on holiday. You might believe they're going to think you're a generous individual, but the actual secondary contact might be that your buddies have a bad opinion on the audience. They may believe you have partners that live on handouts: not at all what the contract was meant to do. The "information distance" returns to certain relational issues, the contrast between what you say when you tell others, and the sense they carry away. So why would it be any different here? Why does a contact discrepancy occur? Language is just the representation of how anything makes you feel. When you have thoughts or encounter stuff in the outside world, emotions are produced. You then bring words together to articulate your feelings and explain what you desire, believe, need, etc. Much of this exists at a subconscious stage, without the need to deliberate over anything you say. The difference exists when describing their internal or emotional feelings; various individuals use different phrases and vocabulary. If you use particular terms and phrases to explain things to another person, certain words and phrases can differ from how they might define the same event themselves. That ensures no one else will encounter or process the vocabulary you use entirely in precisely the same way as you do. Apply to this the reality that no one feels as you do precisely. We also had diverse views, and we viewed the universe differently and our position in it. All have various views and ideals that vary. Your interaction is focused on things that have occurred, things that are occurring or things in existence that you like to happen. Mental thinking is still present, and it is something that differs from person to person. Imagine that as you are heading down the lane, a car pulls out in front of you. The mind processes the event until you inform the passenger something by considering: your beliefs, everything you deem essential in life. What you think people can and shouldn't do while driving and how people can and shouldn't handle each other are your convictions. Your past driving encounters and related circumstances. Your hopes and desires or worrying about what in the case might have happened. There are a lot of potential remarks you may make to your passenger in response after experiencing all of this on a subconscious level. Mentally map yourself back through the first months of dating your new spouse or girlfriend or boyfriend until you learn on. Take a moment to remember how fun and intoxicating it feels to launch this relationship. It's been an exhilarating moment, has it? You were intensely infatuated, even in love already, and it all seemed so simple and perfect. You were totally conscious at the moment while you were with your girlfriend or boyfriend.

It seems like everything about you was disappearing into the past when you just had eyes for each other. You find each other so insanely compelling and attractive that you would shift the heavens and the world as much as possible to be together. Your partner could do no wrong, and you were motivated to bring your best foot forward, with all your blazing beauty, to show your shiniest self. Also, your unexpected eagerness to shed the additional ten pounds to stay in shape could have shocked you. Finally, you began to clean your flat so that your girlfriend or boyfriend wouldn't assume that you were a slob. Or you gave up smoking, starting wearing better clothes, or formed a strong interest in the chosen sport of your girlfriend or boyfriend, all because you wanted to please him or her and prove how dedicated you were to this new relation. Miraculously loosened the vise grasp on your willpower and determination by unsavory behaviors that were once deeply enshrined in your existence. Your partner's simple perception was enough to ignite the fire under you to be a better man or woman. Any previous hesitation in working on ambitions and ventures has given way to a fresh momentum to make something work in your life, items that your wife would find desirable and appealing. If it could only be bottled with this "fresh love tool." Suppose it had lasted a century, rather than a few months. If only we could return to those original euphoric emotions and enthusiasm that pushed us to lift mountains at will. Now to the present day, let's fast-forward. It could be five, ten, twenty, or even fifty years after you begin dating for the first time. You and your wife enjoy each other, but your original infatuation has faded away. Distraction, repetition, and maybe any inattention or apathy have substituted the thrill. Your answer would obviously be different from theirs if they were driving. With a distinct language attached to it, the same external occurrence creates a different answer. To various entities, terms signify different things and overlap under different circumstances. It's more about how various things are interpreted by you. Your perceptions lead you to use those phrases and vocabulary, but you can never be sure if your views are reflected with the person you are referring to. That's why the trust divide is still there. Why is it that the same incident may be observed by two individuals who end up with entirely different interpretations? As per Neuro-Linguistic Programming, the subconscious selectively siphons off the data it is bombarded by while you encounter something in the real universe, to about five and nine items that it will at every point pay heed to. The stuff you siphon off is going to be different than the ones most people do. We prefer to notice the items that are or represent the worldview that is more important to us.

That's why two persons may go to the same event and have a completely different experience: in the same setting, they see different items. Let's assume the Individual A is afraid to be at a football match because the audience could be nervous. He is more inclined to find people who are frowning because of his preconceptions regarding the situation. Individual B goes to the same match wanting people to be polite and comfortable. He has a better likelihood of noticing smiling and laughter. You might have had this feeling if you've ever owned a vehicle. You would occasionally if ever, see the exact car on the road after you have picked the create, model and color you choose. Your subconscious doesn't think that you are important to the things you like. However, when you actually get the vehicle, you continue to see comparable ones everywhere! Either the world wanted to throw more of a tone out there just to frustrate you, or it was already there, and you really didn't see it. So, what's been changing? Now that you have the automobile, your subconscious sees identical ones as incredibly important, because they appear in the "five to nine items" that your consciousness is actually processing. Both of us are special. And when faced by the same external stimuli, we view the environment differently. No wonder, so many of us feel uncertain when it comes to beginning discussions. Communication is a minefield, but your potential, prosperity and satisfaction rely on your relationship with other persons, and that's where this book comes in.

Chapter 1: Basics of Communication and Relationships

Most people will accept that many of the most meaningful events of which we partake are communicative. In large part, our capacity to build and maintain our social life relies on how effectively we interact. The social skills of individuals, personally and socially, are essential to their wellbeing. It is not necessary to overstate the significance of knowing skillful actions with all its nuances. For researchers and laypeople alike, contact systems are a subject of interest. On the one side, our mutual propensity for reviewing, describing, and denouncing this distinctly human practice is noteworthy for its persistent existence (being the target of two centuries of documented analytical scrutiny), and on the other, for the panoply-specific occurrences, metaphysical viewpoints, and theoretical constructs brought on through this effort. And yet, across the centuries and through the continuum of thinking, there is a thread that runs across all this activity. The principle that communicating can be performed "right" or "wrong" and ability development, the belief that people, appropriately equipped or qualified, will come to "do it better." This unifying principle is a concern with abilities. The emphasis on communication skills is certainly attributable, in part, to the reality that most

communicating is a proactive enterprise aimed at executing a variety of realistic tasks (e.g., securing arrangements to settle military wars between countries, simply transmitting knowledge in the classroom, gaining votes in common polls, consoling a sad partner, protecting one 's property and independence in courts. The value of communication skills, though, does not derive solely from the impact they wield in achieving these unique, situation-bound targets. Professional performance, marital happiness, emotional gratification, psychological wellbeing, and even physical wellbeing rely on the individual's social contact abilities, and those of his or her colleagues and interlocutors within these narrower ends. In view of the value of communication skills, it is not shocking that academics and researchers from several backgrounds, including nearly every division of communication (e.g., interpersonal, community, corporate, educational, general, mass), many fields of psychology (cognitive, social, clinical, developmental, and industrial), as well as many fields of psychology (cognitive, social, clinical, developmental, and industrial) have become the continuing focus of analysis. Scholars research public speaking, community interaction, listening, reasoning, dispute management, explanation, corporate leadership, mutual service, relationship management, and on and on, always with a view to making

others grow more easily to do this stuff. The people of this planet join together in the biblical tale of the Tower of Babel to create a structure that would hit heaven. Their attempts fell to naught in a single strike when they were besieged by confused contact, culminating in teamwork breaking down. Owing to inadequate verbal communication capacity, the intended meaning is always miscommunicated, mistaken, misquoted or often skipped entirely. A significant attribute is the ability to interact with other people efficiently. People gain some comprehension of each other through conversation, grow to like each other, affect each other, develop morale, and grow more about themselves and how people view them. People who collaborate successfully know how flexibly, skillfully, and professionally to engage with others, but without compromising their own interests and dignity.

1.1 What Is Communication?

By concept, communication is the transition from one location to another of knowledge. In relationships, contact helps you to clarify what you are feeling and what your desires are about someone else. Not only does the process of communication help to fulfill your desires, but it also encourages you to remain linked in your relationship.

Communicating Clearly in a Relationship

Talk to each other. You cannot interpret the mind of your partner, no matter how much you meet and respect each other. To prevent misunderstandings that may trigger damage, frustration, disappointment or uncertainty, we need to communicate explicitly. It requires two people to have a relationship, and each individual has various requirements and modes of communicating. Couples ought to find a way that fits their relationship to connect. Safe forms of communication include preparation and rigorous work. Connection all the way can never be fine. Be transparent while talking with your spouse, such that it is easy to obtain and comprehend your letter. Double-check your knowledge of what your companion does. If you have a debate with your girlfriend or boyfriend, try to:

- Set aside time to chat without interference from other individuals or disruptions such as telephones, laptops or TV.

- Talk about what you want to say.

- Be explicit about what you intend to say.

- Keep the point simple, so the wife understands it right and knows what you say.

- Speak regarding what happens and how it affects you.

- Using 'I' phrases such as 'I need,' 'I want' and 'I feel' to speak about what you want, need and feel.

- Accepting accountability for your thoughts

- Listen to your partner.

- For the moment, set your feelings away and strive to consider their motives, fears, expectations and expectations (this is called empathy)

- Share with your partner optimistic thoughts, such as what you love and respect about them and how valuable they are to you.

- Know the tone of voice

- Negotiate and note that all the way, you should not have to prove perfect.

- Try to let the topic go, or agree to differ if the concern you are having is not relevant.

Non-verbal communication

We can miss a number of things without communicating while we talk. Meaning is conveyed through our body position, tone of voice and gestures on our face. The other party will be shown through these non-verbal forms of contact how we feel about them. It is always the non-verbal contact that gets 'seen' and accepted if our emotions don't match our sentences. For instance, in a bland, bored tone of voice, saying 'I love you' to your partner offers two very distinct signals. Note what to: you are doing is mirrored in your body language.

Listening and Communication

A very large aspect of good conversation is listening. A strong listener will inspire their spouse to communicate frankly and freely. Includes suggestions for effective listening:

- Maintain convenient eye contact if it is culturally appropriate.

- Lean into the direction of other individual and give gestures to demonstrate attention and concern.

- With the arms and legs uncrossed, create a clear, non-defensive, very comfortable stance.

- Face the other guy, do not sit or stand sideways.

- To stop gazing up or down on the other guy, sit or stand at the same place.

- Prevent disruptive movements like fidgeting with a pen, staring at documents, or clicking your foot or fingers

- Be mindful that effective contact can be challenging due to physical obstacles, disturbances or interruptions. To guarantee that you are listening, silence phones or other contact devices.

- Let the other person talking uninterruptedly.

- Demonstrating real concern and engagement

- Using assertive sentences such as' I see... About ...," "All I need is ...

- Show consideration to tone.

- If you get particularly irritated over something, be willing to take some time off. Before you answer the problem, it may be easier to calm down.

- Seek input from the other party on your listening.

Improving communication in a relationship

It is possible to practice Clear and transparent communication. Some people find it daunting to articulate and will require patience and support to share their thoughts. These individuals may be effective listeners, or they may be individuals whose acts talk louder than their voices. To strengthen your contact, you can benefit by: Building companionship: expressing your partner's perspectives, preferences and worries and displaying love and gratitude. Sharing-intimacy is not just about romantic relationships. By getting moments of feeling near and connected to your spouse, intimacy is established. It implies being able to be relaxed and secure and accessible and frank. An affection gesture may be as easy as taking a cup of tea to your companion when you can see they're tired. To enhance the way you connect, begin by asking questions such as:

- What items are creating tension between you and your partner? Is that, so you don't listen to one another?

- What items gave you pleasure and bonding feelings?

- What stuff cause you discomfort and disappointment?

- What stuff are you not concerned about, and what keeps you from concerned about them?

- How would you want the contact to be different from the partner?

If necessary, ask your spouse these questions and compare your answers. Find and seek strategies to connect differently. See if the contact is strengthened by the observations. You would be able to gain a greater say of what occurs with you as you are more mindful of how you interact. Although it might not be simple at first, opening up different contact fields will contribute to a relationship that is more satisfying.

Some things are difficult to communicate

Any experiences or subjects are uncomfortable for most of us to write about. It could be something that makes one feel awkward, or that is painful. Some people, for instance, find it challenging to communicate their feelings. Sometimes, it is the stuff that cannot be addressed that hurt the worst. If you have trouble explaining yourself or communicating about things with your family, you might find that communicating with a psychologist helps.

Managing conflict with communication

Tips for how to handle contract disputes include:

- Stop the usage of quiet counseling.

- Do not spring to assumptions. Instead of wondering about the causes, find out all the truth.

- Discuss what arose. Hey, don't condemn.

- Learn to accept one another, not to defeat one another.

- Use the future and present tense to communicate, not the past tense.

- Focus on the big thing, and don't get confused by other trivial concerns.

- Speak regarding the topics that affect the feelings of your or your spouse, or pass on to topics with discrepancies of views.

- Using declarations of 'I believe,' not comments of 'You are.'

Seeking help for communication issues

Consider meeting with a relationship coach if you can't seem to boost intimacy in your relationship. Counselors are qualified to identify the habits that trigger difficulties in a couple's relationship and to help improve certain trends, as well as to include solutions, tips and a comfortable space to discuss issues. You might even recommend taking a course specific to your relationship. It's easier to behave early and chat through your problems with others, rather than wait before things worsen.

1.2 Basics of Good Communication

The principles of effective conversation are quite much the same, whether you're a counselor, a salesperson, or just a concerned partner or acquaintance. Two activities, listening and communicating, require good communication, and there are five basic rules for both. This seems pretty simple, but often people overlook that listening and talking are involved in effective conversation. It may also be suggested that the most critical of the two is listening: how do you decide what to suggest until you first consider what the listener wishes or requires or can hear?

Learn to Listen

A two-way street is a collaboration. It is as critical as what we hear about listening efficiently while you are in a discussion, being questioned, or involved in a group. Your focus appears to move from the problem itself to your interactions in the circumstance when you feel nervous. In other terms, you become conscious of how you behave, and you tend to worry about how the signs of distress are apparent to the other people in the room and whether you are unfairly regarded by certain individuals. You become less conscious of various facets of the scenario at the same moment, like what other people mean. This lack of emphasis on what others are thinking will deepen your frustration about whether your answers are acceptable. Sometimes, you can be only marginally conscious of what is being discussed, except you believe you are attentive. There are also fines for not listening. Next, crucial details that the other entity is attempting to share may be overlooked. Only the portions of the message that are aligned with your nervous views can be understood, thereby-your fear. For starters, if you just hear the derogatory remarks of your manager and lack his or her appreciation after a performance review, you would feel poorer than if you had heard the whole appraisal. Not knowing the whole message may also cause you to react improperly, often to something different than what was said. In comparison, the other party may feel like what is being stated is not listening to you. Consequently, the individual could view you as aloof, disturbed, or bored by the discussion.

Blocks to Effective Listening in Messages

A variety of common variables that also conflict with our capacity during discussions, gatherings, debates, and other kinds of social experiences to respond to others. Of these, when people feel uncomfortable in a social setting, five are extremely frequent. These blocks of listening contain the following:

Comparing yourself to the other person

As a means to measure our conduct and results, we all equate ourselves to others. Excessive social anxiety, though, can be correlated with the propensity to do this more regularly, to make negative associations (for example, similarities with others in a single level that are more successful), and to feel terrible after making those associations. This propensity to draw superficial distinctions when conversing interferes with the willingness to respond to and consider what is being discussed (for example, judging yourself with unspoken remarks such as, "I'm not as clever as he is" or "She's more beautiful than I am").

Filtering what the other person says

Filtering means just listening to some aspects of what the other entity is doing. This may mean paying attention only to certain aspects of the interaction in social anxiety that appear to suggest that the other individual is hostile or judgmental.

Rehearsing what to say next

If people are too anxious during discussions or interactions about expressing the correct thing, they sometimes verbally rehearse how they can react to the remarks of other people rather than actually listening to what is being said. While you should participate in rehearsals and make sure that you say the correct thing, this technique can have the reverse impact if done too frequently.

Derailing the conversation

Derailing means shifting the focus of discussion as it becomes either dull or unpleasant. In social anxiety, as the discussion moves into anxiety-provoking areas, derailing can occur. For instance, if you are questioned about your weekend by a coworker, and you are ashamed to confess that you stayed home alone all weekend, you might switch the subject back to a work-related issue instead of sharing what you think is excessively personal details. Derailing will make the other party feel as though you are not sensitive to the topic or are not involved.

Placating the other person

In an attempt to minimize future confrontation, placating means agreeing with the other party regardless of what he or she does. Since fear of being hated or unfairly perceived is correlated with social anxiety, people who are socially insecure frequently go out of their way to comply with others. Many individuals don't plan to see anyone side with them all the time, though. If you always approve with whatever is said, it might increase the doubts of the other party as to whether you are actually listening.

1.3 Improving Your Listening Skills

There are a lot of approaches to develop your communication ability. Instead of just sitting passively and processing the results, successful communication may first require active engagement. Active listening requires ensuring sufficient eye contact, paraphrasing what the individual has said ("so, in other phrases, what you are suggesting is..."), asking for clarity (asking questions to help you appreciate what was meant), and giving input (or the responses to what he or she meant) to the other party. Feedback should be instant (as soon as you recognize the interaction), frank (reflecting your own feelings), and respectful (in other words, respectful and reluctant to harm the other person) wherever possible. Besides, listening with empathy is critical. Being empathic involves conveying the feeling that you fully grasp the message of the other individual as well as the thoughts he or she feels. There are several distinct forms of viewing a specific circumstance, as mentioned. You would be more able to respond and to express the reality when attempting to consider the viewpoint of another person. Notice that you do not need to identify with the viewpoint of the other party, only to consider it. However, even though anyone mentions anything that you think is totally false, at least a tiny portion of the statement that is valid will possibly be detected.

Even if you don't agree with the general substance of what has been expressed, having the user realize that you appreciate his or her experience conveys empathy. Eventually, good listening involves listening to transparency and consciousness. Openness means listening while failing to locate the fault. Awareness includes

- Understanding how a conversation fits in with your own information and perceptions and how a contact fits in with your own.

- Being mindful of any differences, such as sound, stance, and facial gestures, in the spoken message itself and the nonverbal dimensions of the conversation.

1.4 Purpose of Communication in Relationships

One of the main relationship issues is that most spouses have a profound misunderstanding of what the object of conversation is. Most of the solution is to speak to a partner as a dialogue in which everyone offers a preconceived version of the truth of what is occurring between the two partners. The problem with this technique is the incorrect belief that, with an honest understanding of the fact, any participant will move through the discussion. This is not feasible since neither entity has the requisite knowledge, that is, what is going on between them, to decide what truth is. One aim of communicating is to decide what truth is. Cooperation requires two people's relationships as they express and discuss all their experiences, emotions, suggestions and opinions and come to a clear interpretation of what is going on.

Collaborative Communication

Everybody acknowledges that conversation is merely a question of communicating and listening. Most of us, though, falsely think that the issue of communication is easy. Instead of including natural talents, we tend to understand that conversation requires new skills that can be taught and built-in ourselves to speak to and respond to our loved ones.

Approaching a Conversation with Your Relationship Partner

When entering into a discussion with your partner, guideline number one to follow: immediately disarm. Giving up the desire to prove right, that is. You don't head through a war where you've got to fight. This does not mean you're going to have to negotiate or capitulate. This is not to suggest that you will not be irritated, upset or triggered. You have a right to all the opinions and emotions you have. Only remember that there might be something your companion has to suggest that it is worth listening to and contemplating. This debate is not a battlefield where you have to show you're right; it's not a war you have to win.

Talking to Your Relationship Partner

There is only one truth that a person should be confident about before entering into a conversation: you should recognize what your own emotions, feelings and perceptions are. You may be assured about nothing else: not the emotions, opinions or expectations of the other person, not even the truth of what is occurring between the two of you. The only thing you ought to add to the table with your spouse is something that both of you will be confident of: your own opinions, emotions, and perceptions. Talking personally regarding yourself, though, is always more complex than you would expect.

Focus on yourself

It is an inconvenient fact that one partner is abused by the other in almost all couples. As a consequence, accusing each other is the subject of much of their conversations. Avoid the urge to slip into attacking, threatening, insulting or dismissing your companion in your attempt to communicate about yourself. You're going to talk to you. Not about your wife, or the kids, or your partners or job. Only for you. What are you trying to think for yourself? Look at your companion and reflect on what, at this moment, you should show to him-her of yourself.

Reveal feelings that are embarrassing or humiliating.

Recognizing your unreasonable emotions is critical. Don't ignore them as unacceptable, childish or irrelevant. Allow an attempt to speak through the thoughts you'd rather gloss through. Should you reveal them, the emotions that you assume may bring you shame or humiliation. For starters, address these feelings with your spouse if you feel upset or frustrated. By being abused and righteous, resist the urge to protect yourself. This is not about how sad or upset you shouldn't be. It's all about the plain fact that you're upset or frustrated, and the physical distress is triggered by it.

Reveal your personal wants.

People sometimes feel guilty about what they intend to chat

about. It's not easy: I want to go to a new restaurant. I want a new sweater; I want to go on a journey. But the specific wishes that come from the heart of you, where you feel the most vulnerable: I want you to compliment me, I want you to be affectionate, I want you to have a child. There are some of us who have grown up feeling guilty about our urges. The better you connect at this stage, though, the deeper you are in contact with yourself, the more honest you are as an entity, the closer your spouse may be able to connect to you. On this specific basis, as you and your wife connect, all of the insignificant problems within you dissolve. It becomes obvious that in your relationship, they were simply inconsequential concerns designed to distract you.

Communicate with your companion with the integrity and reverence

Many people have a particular way to interact that they reserve with their spouses. What makes it unique is that dysfunctional habits are included, such as moaning, challenging, bossy, irritable, rude, immature, paternal, condescending, to name a couple. "Stop and question yourself while you're talking to your partner:" Will I be talking to someone else like this? Can you find yourself moaning (I'm too tired) or asking (Get me a drink of water) or deferring (What am I going to get for dinner?)

in situations that you seldom learn from most people? After all, your partner is another human attempting to treat your partner with the dignity and fairness of which you regard every other human.

Listening to Your Relationship Partner

You have so little understanding of what your companion actually believes and experiences while entering into a discussion. You may say you're doing that because you know the word he or she still gets when he-she gets injured. Or maybe you've even shared a few tense terms. Yet you know absolutely nothing before you've spoken to your buddy. Listening is an ability that needs to be established and mastered. Only because we are alert doesn't mean we are aware. We will really get to know the person only when we listen with an unconditional curiosity in knowing the person who is talking to us.

Listening is not about you.

Listening is solely about the person about which you are listening. Place your point of view back. Your views, ideas or comments are both unrelated and inappropriate to what the other person is doing. The person who is talking is not asking for help or encouragement from you. What they just need is to be understood in order to know they're being noticed.

Hear your partner out

When you set yourself away, you make yourself open to listening to your partner when you concentrate on what your partner is thinking rather than to how you are responding. Try to sense what it sounds like to be him-her when your companion speaks. Try to feel what you are doing with your partner. Only empathize. Through your core, listen. Try to feel like he feels in the case as he relates an event to you. Make a particular attempt when interacting for you to empathize with what your companion is actually doing.

Indicate that you are hearing your partner

Listening secretly is not enough. It is beneficial to reassure your companion that you are listening to him or her. Throughout the talk, remember what the companion is doing and experiencing. Speak to him — it's what you hear — it's what you think and what you believe it's what you believe. Your companion will correct you if your reflection is not true. Once you have a clear interpretation of what your companion is attempting to convey to you, you should then create changes. Reflecting helps your partner to realize that he is being noticed, and lets him feel understood by you.

Have compassion for your partner

When you listen with respect to your companion and

understand what he or she thinks, you develop compassion for him or her as a human. As a human being with emotional suffering and challenges like the majority of us, you care for him-her. You get a fresh outlook. Your own emotional over-reactions to them appear unimportant when you talk about your partner's problems. It appears condescending and patronizing to immediately offer suggestions or be judgmental. Suddenly, behaving injured or abused becomes juvenile and self-indulgent. From this viewpoint, when she struggles with her own challenges in life, you see your wife as a different person than you care deeply for.

Determine Reality with Your Relationship Partner

It is possible that you also come to a better understanding of what you were doing and contemplating in the course of individually sharing to yourself while your companion actually listened. Similarly, when your companion communicated personally to you of you genuinely listening, both of you most definitely come to a better comprehension of the perceptions and thoughts of your spouse. In addition to the emotions of empathy and sympathy that surround it, this degree of wisdom and comprehension helps explain many of the uncertainty that remains between the pair. Many of the assumptions, misinterpretations and miscommunications that cause this misunderstanding are removed through greater knowledge of each other. A better understanding of yourself and of the truth of your relationship is what remains. You and your partner might want to examine what you have learned about yourself and each other and about your relationship at this point in the discussion. You will recognize the personal challenges and responses that appear to contribute to trouble amongst you by sharing what you have experienced. You will now know what to watch out for in the future to escape problems. And if you fall into problems with each other, you will understand what's going on more easily and cope with it.

Helpful Advice about Communication

There are some detrimental ways of behavior to be conscious of. Be sure that you should not participate in all of these, so the contact mechanism is tainted by them. You may be confident that you and your wife will grow increasingly separated and estranged from each other as long as you employ these tactics. The connection should get you closer to each other and your spouse. It can be used not to set up fortifications between you, but to knock down the walls that hold you apart.

1.5 Principle of First Response

The course of a confrontation is not decided by the individual starting it, but by the party reacting to it. When you don't hear anything that you want, how do you react? You may believe it's all right to verbally strike someone because "He/she is choosing a battle with me." You may be right, but that entity does not have the ability to determine if a battle eventually exists. The power resides on the answerer, you.

Principle of Physical Touch

It is hard to injure anyone when you are touching him or her tenderly. A tough period for this theory to be implemented is when a debate has started. An ideal moment, though, is when you realize you are going to sit down and hold a conversation about something that might contribute to stress.

Proper Timing

A discussion's effectiveness will be maximized if the pacing of the discussion is deliberately picked. There are moments when it becomes important to hold a discussion at a particular moment. Yet much of the time, the pacing of our discussions can be more deliberate.

Mirroring

If we test it often in dialogue, comprehension will be strengthened. We must make careful to incline our ears if we are to learn and grow wise. Did you ever say one thing about what you said, but anything different was understood by the person you were referring to? This can make for a very frustrating conversation. If you're not sure whether your spouse gets what you're talking about, try to see if you hear a tonne of this phrase: "What do you say by that?" Mirroring will help you assess if your spouse is adequately understood. Once an argument is raised by the partner ... reiterate that to him or her. Say anything like this: "So, what I hear you say is ..." or, "Are you thinking ...?" And tell your partner, with your own terms, what you think that you understand. Then, there is the most critical aspect of mirroring. Your partner must be permitted to either confirm or correct what you have written. The purpose of mirroring is not to prove right, not to protect yourself, but to recognize that you are listening correctly. If you are seeking to learn rather than making yourself known, so with this theory, you are equipped for success.

Prayer

When we welcome a universal force, or someone greater than oneself to be an involved participant and guide, progress in conversation is more possible. This idea is not complex, but it needs our close attention. We have been so used to thinking about prayer that its value sometimes passes us by. No matter what idea you might use at the moment or what subject you might be dreaming about, no condition is beyond prayer. In our contact with each other, we can finally and ultimately suggest something false. The theory that many lose in war is because they hesitate until the hour of war. The explanation that some win is that, long before the war arrived, they earned their triumph on their knees. Anticipate your battles; combat them on your knees until temptation arrives, and victory will all be yours. One of the main obstacles that couples experience with this principle is awkwardness. Together, they are not accustomed to prayer. So, in the middle of unconstructive contact, when they tend to like each other less, the idea of praying together is not quite enticing; however, you can start little. The single most valuable person you have in your life should be your wife. Connection, like it or not, is the instrument that has been entrusted to humanity to knit our hearts and minds together. If we're able to apply any conscious concepts, progress is probable. With modesty and trust, move ahead. We concentrate more exclusively on what we do not like when we are upset, and our thinking is wrapped up in images of the wrongness of those concerned. We've lost sight of what we desire and still need. You will learn how to alter this trend and interact with the life-serving intent of rage utilizing the above-mentioned measures. You're going to figure out where frustration stems from and discover how to communicate it in ways that suit your needs as well as others' needs. Use these measures during an angry confrontation to re-focus your efforts and learn to produce results that are meaningful for all concerned.

1.6 Communication Skills Every Couple Should Develop

When intimacy difficulties tend to overtake their relationship, it's very normal for spouses to seek counseling. Do you get the gut feeling as if you and your wife are already withholding something from each other? Or does it feel like your companion really doesn't see you anymore? Maybe you like you've been really straightforward on your viewpoint because it's the issue with your companion that from your point of view, they really can't seem to grasp the problems. Blaming each other for what doesn't succeed, while enticing, won't bring you the happiness you crave so badly. Whether you strive together to overcome a tough scenario or everyday disagreements have become the standard, the better collaboration will help all. To help you move on a better road to shared understanding and a deeper relation, here are some tips:

Choose an appropriate moment to address the problems peacefully

Preserving time for each other to check-in will help you be more effective. In the immediate future, schedule a moment when you are all going to be relaxed and happy. You could notice that you prefer to function better in the morning, or Sunday afternoon, when you're in a more comfortable mood. You could need to somewhat change the timetable so that you have any spare time. Very many, when it's happening, couples try to address a problem. Although this might not work sometime, it will allow you to be more comfortable and accessible with your spouse by offering each other a heads-up to explore things more in-depth. Take a minute to articulate the need and then, at a more fitting period, follow up with a recommendation. It conveys appreciation and concern, which tends to cultivate a token of goodwill between two people.

Understand and Communicate your partner's perspective

Listening may be challenging, especially when the other individual says something that causes a protective reaction in you. Remind yourself that you're going to have a turn as well; it's important to check in right now and not disturb. Keep eye contact with your companion and be completely present. By concentrating solely on the interaction and what's being discussed, you will illustrate being aware. Instead of one party being "right" or "wrong," it may be useful to consider the conversation as having two contradictory views. If you're not certain regarding anything, pose a reflective question or two and make sure you fully understand. Maybe you might even say, "Am I having that right?" or, "I want to be sure I understand; tell me if I hear you right" Take turns talking to each other and listening. It will make a substantial change to invest only 10 minutes concentrating on the other individual expressing their experience. Take a 5-minute break if you think things are growing, then come back.

Be mindful of your language and Tone

Missing a significant meaning may be too simple because we don't like the sound with which something is being spoken. Take stock. Stop yourself as you have the need to become accusatory or to start a sentence with "You still ...". Only remind yourself what you're doing right now, instead of being aggressive or accused, taking a minute to calm down before answering helps you express what you really feel. "You could attempt, perhaps:" Learning about this only tends to lead us down a dangerous road. I would like to get with it to a new position, but I'm just not sure how. This sort of declaration might help enable a more meaningful discussion. If you learn that a specific subject is extremely complicated, it may help to express your thoughts about the situation. For instance, you might say, "I'd really like to speak to you about (the problem), but I'm worried about it because I know that this is an environment we tend to struggle with." This kind of comment will also ease the burden to get it right the first time. Be gentle with yourself; contact with your spouse will become more fruitful with time and practice.

Think in terms of what you have to offer. Don't be only concerned with what you can take

While all give and take are definitely very good relationships, as both parties are concentrated on sharing, they improve their capacity to manage conflict more effectively. You may change a troublesome situation with any enhanced understanding. Tune more cautiously into your speech and acts. Is there anything that you should tell or do better to achieve specific outcomes? We give a loving message to our spouse when we are compassionate, and we will work from a position of generosity and compassion when we feel cared for. What constructive and distinctive traits can you add to your relationship? What makes you so lucky to have your wife with you? Why are you going to react to the condition positively?

Note and express what you value in your partner

All wishes to be accepted and admired. It may be quick to slip into a thought habit of: "I feel like I do too much, but no one cares." We cultivate an environment of moral kindness when we take the time to publicly acknowledge the positive attributes and good works of everyone else. See anything you are thankful for with your partner? Be on the alert to say what you would enjoy. Sometimes, we prefer to dwell in relationships on what we don't have or what's not going. All the differences can be achieved with this vital change in attitude to an emphasis on the optimistic. You may notice your companion is starting to show their love for how amazing you are, too. Take the time to analyze and consider the viewpoint of your spouse and reflecting that you actually "get it" will have a huge influence on your relationship's longevity. Check out the above tips the next time you find yourself a little lost, to help you step into a stronger, more rewarding relationships.

Chapter 2: Couples Communication and Intimacy

If you're really in love with your childhood darling, so it will last for a long time. Unfortunately, not so many of us have had a privileged encounter. There are several kinds of relationships, and we have certainly read of or witnessed plenty of them ourselves by the time we've entered our 40s+. What are the thoughts that the term 'relationship' gives to you? Security, protection, support and comfort? Stress, enmity, terror, suffering, sacrifice? Considering just what type of intimacy you desire, more of will be useful when dreaming about intimacy and the aspects of your relationship that you want to strengthen. In relationship intimacy, the five facets are:

Emotional intimacy

Of the emotional communication, to be equal. That could mean moaning or yell at the same kinds of things, or that you are also similarly responsive or emotionally resilient.

Intellectual intimacy

Being on the same frequency. You exchange opinions and insights and feel worthy of knowing the thinking patterns of each other.

Physical intimacy

By reciprocal contact, sensuality and sexual satisfaction, being connected physically and sharing a common connection.

Recreational intimacy

Being willing, by common needs and preferences in non-essential pursuits, to joke, smile and have fun together.

Spiritual intimacy

Being willing to share the major stuff with degrees of enthusiasm and fervor that are comparable. It may be faith, politics, environmental concerns, civil rights, animal rights, or simply expressing a passionate belief in almost nothing.

Settling Arguments and Conflicts with your Partner

Disagreements are faced by any couple. Couples will overcome their disagreements in a constructive manner and understand more about each other when treated with consideration, empathy and comprehension. Couples will easily become separated and forced away and not properly resolved.

Identifying your argument style

Finding out how to react to a disagreement between you and your spouse will help you consider how disputes evolve.

Subtle subversive

Tendencies to prevent conflict and sometimes through silence, nagging or moaning points at difficulties. The issue is always the lengthy construction that occurs before an argument breaks out.

High-level attacker

Also vocal during a disagreement and dominating. They could have come from contexts where noisy and repeated claims have been made, and therefore see this style as natural.

Pre-emptive striker

It dislikes blow-ups and tries to discourage a full-scale war in all ways. It may be a fragile and protective disposition.

Shock absorber

Fearing claims, he/she declines to participate in a row, at least in some direction. Unvoiced anger and animosity will reside under the surface.

Peace-seeking missive

Dislikes tension and attempts as soon as possible to stop a row. This will distract from working on addressing the source of the dispute. It may be hard for a pair to communicate successfully during a dispute as various models' clash. The main point to reflect on is to approach the challenge as the opponent and to see yourself in arms as comrades. Here are few early warning indicators of the brewing of a conflict:

- You prevent communication with the eyes, physical affection and sex.

- You recruit or challenge your companion for anything.

- You reply with quick, curt answers to attempts at conversation.

- Your emotions dwell on the bad aspects of your partner.

2.1 Types of Couples

Researchers have been able to categorize couples into five groups, drawing from over four decades of study results. Each form is somewhat distinct from the others, and it has its advantages and dangers for each form of couple.

Conflict Avoiders

Conflict avoiders reduce efforts at persuasion and stress their places of the shared ground instead. They prevent confrontation, prevent voicing what they need from each other, and praise their relationship for being content in general. The balance between individuality and interdependency is an essential feature of conflict-avoiding couples. They have strong borders and are distinct entities with distinct preferences. This is not to denigrate the success of the places where they meet and depend on each other. In certain regions of overlap, where they are interdependent, they may be very related and loving.

Volatile Couples

Volatile partners are almost the complete opposite of confrontation avoiders, deeply emotional. They automatically begin persuasion during a dispute debate, and they keep to it during the conversation. A tone of fun, mutual enjoyment, and satire are defined by their discourse. They seem to love to discuss and discuss, but they are not rude and provocative. However, there can be a lot of expressed detrimental consequences, like frustration and feelings of vulnerability, but no scorn. Around their individual universes, they have no defined borders, and there is considerable overlap. While they have to dispute a great deal over their positions, in their conversation, they stress link and integrity.

Validating Couples

These couples' interaction is marked by comfort and relaxation. They are very vocal, but neutral for the most part. They tend to be transitional, in certain cases, between avoiders and explosive partners. They place a lot of focus on supporting and recognizing the point of view of their spouse and are also empathic with the emotions of their spouse. They are going to confront their disagreements, but just on those issues and not on others. In certain topics, they may become intensely aggressive and may transform into a power fight. Typically, they then settle down and negotiate. Validating pairs are only slightly emotionally expressive during the confrontation.

Hostile Couples

Hostile couples are like couples being validated, such that all parties have elevated levels of defensiveness.

Hostile-Detached Couples

These couples are like warring factions with no definite victor, just a stale-partner, engaged in a mutually exhausting and desolate confrontation. During the confrontation, they snipe at each other, but the air is full of moral detachment and indifference, similar to gun smoke.

2.2 What sort of relationship you want?

If you're really in love with your childhood darling, so it will last for a long time. Unfortunately, not so many of us have had a privileged encounter. There are several kinds of relationships, and we have certainly read of or witnessed plenty of them ourselves by the time we've entered our 40s+. What are the thoughts that the term 'relationship' gives to you? Security, protection, support and comfort? Stress, enmity, terror, suffering, sacrifice?

Your relationships are about You

The links we draw are a result of the contact we have with ourselves. What we send away, we attract. It affects what we offer away when we adjust. We get what we think we need subconsciously, and then we get what we embrace or tolerate. Consequently, the self-concept forms the life you build for yourself and the relationships you step into. The consistency in relationships can be determined by how you act when you think of the other guy or are with him. When you are around them, how you behave for yourself defines the emotions you desire and plan to get. Either our relationships shift with us, or we may wish to discard them when they have become like a snake's skin that restrains and constricts.

A great relation has great communication.

Check out the foundations

We must first analyze the roots while searching for a new relationship, both our own and those of our prospective spouse. We may decide if previous interactions have established psychological structures that are either shaky or solid. But our pillars support our limitations and how robust and welcoming we are in our experiences. If each person has a background of violence or negligence, so their pillars will be less robust, and they will be less likely to accept that any emotional storms will pass. In the relationship, they can produce their own storms, measure the foundations, and reassure themselves with either their protection and power or affirm their instability.

Choosing to be without a romantic relationship

You might know a couple of female partners who have no inclination to be back in a relationship. In their adult relationships with guys, they had such a stormy period that they decided to remain single to stop some more emotionally-draining dramas. Tired and extremely dissatisfied with men in general, they have been. Their children grew up and, maybe, brought them the pleasure of their grandchildren. They see an incentive for their human right to be associated with those through peer communities such as book and film clubs. Most people have their own financial resources and stability, which they do not wish to jeopardize by living with another partner.

Attachment matters

Each of the different kinds of relationships has its own links to the multiple types of relational commitment that we formed in childhood. We are either anticipating or seeking partners with a similar 'attachment type' to our own. Or we are searching for the attributes and attributes we truly appreciate that we miss in ourselves. For once in our lives, we hope that we can then feel full and whole. For similar motives, new future partners may still search out candidates, but no side will yet be conscious of what is guiding their decision. There is a much simpler period in relationships for the most emotionally stable of us. They grew up with trustworthy and trustworthy parents, and they expressed unconditional affection, had simple and stable borders, had meaningful contact, and understood deep down that they were cherished and loved. They were enthusiastic about sharing their lives with someone like them and about expecting this relationship to last. There's another tale of unhappier consequences for the majority of us. If we have grown up without the hope of satisfying our emotional needs, it would be impossible for us to believe anyone. In all of our relationships, getting an unstable attachment style like this will cause us difficulties-and, perhaps result in a choice to be insular, bury the discomfort of our unmet desires, and give up on relationships entirely. We can keep pushing the limits to check the tolerance of someone else for our actions, and we may drive that person away for good by doing so. There might be a desire to replay the old scenario compulsively and the heartbreak of not feeling loved, safe and unique. We do it with the expectation of somehow altering the result of the story as we replicate what is sadly common to us. The expectation is,

'I'll have it right this time.' Further mind-games and power-struggles we fear. We despair of being trapped in certain endlessly repeated loops, complaints and the acute anxiety and discomfort of rejection or alienation in the Groundhog Day drama. Instead of risking being isolated, others would participate in such an emotionally exhausting drama. In such an emotionally manipulative and neglectful relationship, the reality is that they are now emotionally isolated.

Starting again

After being married or dedicated to a relationship for decades, there are individuals that start dating again. We may want the nice fun things out of a new relationship, but we don't want to be bound again to domesticity and obligation. We have an empty nest, and that's how we plan to hold it. There are many people who are profoundly dissatisfied in their current relationships, but since they risk being single and 'on the shelf' in old age, they keep put and settle for a number less than they deserve. There is also a 'positive selfishness' that stems with not needing to be the career of those in old age and finding the time and money to cross off certain things on the bucket list ... With partners of ours. In a new relationship, there will also be a clash in priorities, brought on by a lack of consistent expression about what we want and predict. We make predictions instead, and hope for the best. Our harmony and mutual view of the potential of every new relationship must be assessed. Some of us are not quite aware whether, when it comes to sharing our time and maybe our lives together, a new spouse would be 'on the same page.' Not all of us risk upsetting the boat early on by mentioning explicitly what we are searching for exactly. We don't want to be too fussy or bossy. If they think there's a risk of repelling the future partner, it's a remarkable phenomenon for anyone to be straightforward and up-front with anything. After a few weeks or months, secret realities could then surface, and we have re-evaluated, redefined, and even terminated the relationship. When we are enthusiastically contemplating the possibilities ahead, it is best to be straightforward and assertive at the outset. Early on, set the expectations and borders.

Not all relationships are equal

There's a wide variety of relationships from which we should pick, and they can be discussed with all sides in an educated decision. There are some relationships that neglect mental, physical and sexual affection and tender treatment and where they may feel more suffocating at the other end of the continuum.

If you're completely engulfed in the realm of dating and swiping left and right on Tinder, or you're in a dedicated LTR, just a few hiccups and needless battles here and there. When it comes to dating, we can both use a little space for change. In reality, you should not be left tired, strained, or questioned by your love life. It is meant to leave you satisfied, energized, and empowered. You've got some prep to do if it isn't. Suppose you are single with no intention to settle down, more power to you (although I utterly hate the saying). If you are in a relationship at the moment or are searching for a relationship, here's how to make it your life's best relationship:

2.3 Types of Relationships

Detached

A practical relationship that excludes any personal bonds, such as escorts, one-night stands, and casual flings.

Platonic

While they might be intimate and enjoy the other individual, a relationship of affection and help is not treated as a possible life partner.

Partners with benefits

A fuzzy line without the intention of establishing a stable relationship that involves sexual intimacy.

Loose polygamous

There is a third person, or multiple of them, in the arrangement. Another relationship may be going opposite, or orgies, swinging gatherings, dancers, a 'broken' life as a transvestite and/or even bisexual partners may be desired. There is a private existence for one or both couples that strangers will have no knowledge about. In order not to avoid losing the relationship and being left all alone, maybe one spouse has agreed to accept the actions.

Loose monogamous

A devoted person who do not divide the assets of a household or shared one. They possibly have holidays together, and spend time with the families of each other, have social activities together, and as a group, attend events. Owing to financial or family considerations, or because they risk getting 'trapped' by the repetitive patterns that come with living together with a partner or partner, they may have committed to this form of relationship.

All in

These couples share their life ambitions, their home and income, and whether one works abroad, they might consciously build a mixed family and spend a lot of time together. A couple's traditional portrait.

These fundamental power structures may also occur inside these relationships: -

Parent & Child couples – One is child-like and incompetent (for example, of the organization of the home or finances) while the other is more parent-like and takes charge of their spouse, allowing provisions to compensate for the deficiencies of their spouse. This power differential of dependency and care-taking, or of passivity and superiority, can serve all parties.

Master & Slave – A strong power disparity where both sides will like and embrace, or there would be a struggle for one against the feelings of injustice and obedience to being intimidated.

Two Peas in A Pod – Where a mixed identity occurs, they can complete each other's sentences and wear matching outfits! 'We are like one' is the post. This may sound comfortable or stifling, and when the relationship ends, it causes additional difficulties, particularly when it is due to a bereavement.

Dis-organized & Dramatic – When there are heavy suspense and cynical and derogatory banter. Big fall outs and passionate make-ups might be there. It is on-and-off, push-and-pull, stop-start, suffocating or isolating. A popular roller-coaster of sensations! Wanting others while they are aloof and jaded, but wanting them only before they move to be more intimate.   Too big for warmth. Then follows the development of space to drive them further again by reasons or emotional removal. They can't survive with them, and they can't survive without them.' There may be childhood dramas that reactivate emotions that are unlovable and incapable of time or affection, or that are forgotten, overlooked, mocked or bullied, and that need to feel important and heard in confrontation. Sadly, no one else, but ourselves, will repair the early relationship wounds. We also need to consider our own habits to learn how to respond in ways that get us everything we need to be able to thrive to experience life fully. Our relationships are fundamental to our lives, and we were not taught much about them in education. We had to practice at college. The primary bond we have is still the one we have with ourselves and our inner girl, who wants our affection, empathy, concern, caring and compassion. To be her play partner and defender, her champion and counselor, she wants us. Our inner child's well-being is a barometer of the well-being of our relationships. 'Till death do you part' then he/she has you, and you have them.

2.4 Communication pitfalls to avoid

There are many kinds of stuff you'll want to stop wherever, especially true, when it is related to communication.

The silent treatment

People sometimes tolerate silent treatment, assuming it's establishing limits, but when clearly shared by a spouse, limits work well. Otherwise, they do not understand they have reached them. It is easier to be assertive regarding a barrier than to presume that a spouse recognizes why you are hurting and cuts them out, which can also bring a relationship more pain.

Bringing up past mistakes

During a heated moment, it is easy to slip into the trap of rehashing the past. Dredging up the errors of your companion frequently may be detrimental and only make them more protective.

Yelling or screaming

During a disagreement, raising your voice or resorting to shouting and crying is an inefficient form of processing your frustration. It can trigger disputes to become more intense in the long run and erode the self-esteem of your spouse.

Walking away

Stonewalling or walking away from the center of the dispute is a way to disengage the spouse to leave unanswered disputes. Feeling stressed and having a timeout is reasonable. Make sure to clarify why the discussion needs you to take a momentary pause.

Sarcasm and put-downs

When you're in the middle of debating, be mindful of offensive language. It is easier to make a harmless comment for yourself if you want to crack the ice than to suggest anything derogatory for them.

Disrespectful nonverbal behavior

Volumes may be conveyed through body language. For instance, checking your phone rather than facing it and making eye contact can make the other person feel disrespected.

The bottom line

The cornerstone of a good relationship is efficient communication, but that doesn't mean it's always simple. If you have a tough time functioning in your relationship with the conversation, suggest seeing a psychiatrist, either on your own or through your girlfriend or boyfriend, to sort on the potential difficulties and learn some different resources.

2.5 How to Keep Connected

Maintaining a good sense of attachment is one feature that is vital to any romantic relationship. You feel safe, understood and as though you will overcome the universe together when you are genuinely linked with your spouse. But in the midst of the unbearable stressors of life, how can you sustain the connection? The approach is different than what you would expect when it all boils down to having your spouse fulfill their own specific needs. A relationship is not a place you go to receive, it's a place you go to share, and you can feel a degree of attachment and satisfaction that you have never known before as you reflect on the needs of your spouse as if they were your own. Have you ever felt like you're tip-toeing around your companion on eggshells? No matter what you suggest, should she (or he) get defensive? This problem is simply not a contact question, considering what you would believe.' It's something larger. But, if you both "focus on improved communicating" to fix your difficulties as a team, I hate to break it to you. You're only treating the symptoms. It's the real condition that you need to recognize and resolve in the relationship, else disconnect and tension will occur. When the connection is broken, what happens? A typical end-result of feeling isolated is infidelity unless resolved early. Infidelity is damaging, whether it is physical or mental, and is a challenge that often partners have to struggle with. "The tale is pretty much the same with each affected couple:" I felt lonely," "I felt rejected,"

"I felt afraid," "You didn't seem to worry about me anymore. Although there is no reason for being unfaithful, when they feel isolated, ignored or overlooked in the relationship, it becomes convenient for one to explain infidelity. All connections go through ups and downs, but there might be moments when it feels like you've missed the original spark you've had with your partner, or when you're not as connected anymore. But in your long-term relationship, if you want to sustain a good bond, you certainly will. And also, the evidence is there to back that up. Nevertheless, bear in mind that this is not always anything to think about. For couples to begin to feel bored or like a spark is lacking, it's absolutely natural. People certainly shouldn't feel awkward about it. Good partners, though, are the ones that do much about it. Recognize that if you sound like the flame is fading. And finally, as a pair, determine if you intend to bring that back. To start doing fun/novel stuff together again is the perfect way to recapture the flame. It will impress even the most entrenched/bored couples how easily they start loving their relationships again. We all know that affection sometimes, over time, disappears between a pair. Passion is starting to diminish. Eventually, feelings of togetherness and sincere love will turn into anger and bitterness. You don't want all of this to happen in your relationship, clearly. Couples generally speak to each other about their differences, disputes and misunderstandings in order to fix these problems, each expressing his or her point of view. But these discussions also contribute to intensified feelings of disdain, instead of an attachment. A few suggestions for learning and keeping linked are below.

My Needs Versus Your Needs

If you have ever been on a plane, you realize that you can first put your own oxygen mask on if the cabin pressure decreases, and then support everyone, even your kids. What might happen to your kids, though, if you were ill-prepared to even assist yourself? It could be too late to intervene if you've fumbled for too long to keep your mask on. Although we can first take care of our own needs, staying in a continual state of preparation is the answer as a spouse. Otherwise, each of you would constantly scramble to fulfill your own desires and ignore each other's desires. It is, therefore, necessary to create a distinction between wants and requires, as well as current and potential requirements, in addition to being in a constant state of preparation. Just because you like something doesn't imply it is a necessity, and it doesn't imply it's an urgent requirement just because you have a desire. A simple rule of thumb to obey is to guarantee that your immediate needs are addressed consistently so that you can better with the needs of your spouse when they emerge.

Be more intimate with each other

It can be quick to slip into a rut if you've been with your spouse for a long time and fail to express respect and devotion to one another. And then, in order to remain linked, that is exactly what you need to do. Studies also have shown that the region of our brain known as the frontal orbital cortex lights up when we feel an intimate contact. Touch also encourages oxytocin development, the 'heart hormone' that helps you feel more linked and caring to another. The most you can touch, the stronger. Holding hands, cuddling, hugging. A connection is one of the most influential aspects of a relationship, but as you stroll down the street or stay to opposite ends of the sofa, it's easy to avoid keeping hands as time passes. Create an attempt by utilizing the power of contact to emotionally re-engage with your partner.

Try new things Together

If you have tried something different as a pair for a minute, even if it was just visiting a new place, then it is certainly time to venture beyond your comfort zones. The analysis showed that there was greater fulfillment in their relationships with married couples who invested time engaged in new activities.

In a long-term relationship, especially if you continue to revisit the same restaurants and replicate the same things, there's a real risk of falling into a rut. Yet you can hold the light burning by doing different stuff. The brain's reward mechanism may be activated by new stimuli, allowing hormones such as dopamine and norepinephrine to be published. This is basically the same hormones that are normally produced in the early stages of courtship, but you can chemically replicate the 'spark' that you feel when you first met by stimulating this region of the brain.

Pay less attention to your Phones

It's only normal for both of you to waste time on your own things, like messaging buddies, reading accounts, and simply avoiding each other in favor of technology. You may want to make an attempt to put your phones away on a daily basis to remain linked, however. According to the study, it affects relationship happiness by giving more attention to our phones than to our spouses. It's easy to come home and automatically start scrolling, but this will build a disconnect between you and your loved one over time. To maintain a good relationship, it is not appropriate to say you don't have telephones. However, the amount of time you spent on them can be minimized. For example, consider enforcing 'device-free' hours, no mobile phones after 6 p.m. Alternatively, commit your time to one another. Take part in a chat, attempt to get dinner together, or go on a stroll around the city. Concentrate without any disruptions on being truly present together.

Go on Dates Again

Not just for the joy of getting out of the house, but as a way to maintain your relationship heading in a good direction, it is always necessary to go on dates. There's something in relationship science named 'self-expansion theory. When we start dating for the first time, we don't know anything about each other. We have different preferences and lives. When we attempt different activities together, though, we continue to extend ourselves to involve our colleagues and all the unique opportunities we have together. That's why long-term partners are sometimes recommended by clinicians and consultants to render date nights a focus again. For partners, those new feelings of enthusiasm and novelty are always pleasant. This is particularly valid for activities that couples may do together that are very exciting or novel (e.g., skydiving, escape rooms, difficult obstacle courses). Of course, in order to maintain a flame going, it is not important to leap out of a plane. It can remind you why you came together in the first place if you can have the same sort of fun you had in the early days, and help keep things new.

Share Goals and Dreams with each other

You could quit worrying about your hopes and aspirations, and everything else you look forward to in life until you realize you're together. Yet it's the same thing that brings partners together, and they remain as content as they did on the first day. Share the visions of success with each other, and work together to carry them forward. These might be long-term proposals, such as owning a house in France or backpacking in the Andes, but that doesn't imply that you can't explore them together and appreciate the dream. Really, doing so can also bring to your relationship some much-needed excitement. It is a profoundly bonding feeling to help and express the aspirations of your spouse and will hold the romance and affection alive in your relationship for the long term.

Figure out your Love Languages

It might be time to work out your love languages and reflect on them in your relationship if it seems like you've been distant lately. There are numerous forms that individuals choose to give and accept affection. These involve words of encouragement, acts of support, gift-giving, sharing time together on education, and physical contact. Figuring out the vocabulary of your affection, as well as your partner's, will always make all the difference in the universe. You will produce the products depending on them because you recognize the desires of your spouse. Do they require reinforcement phrases? You will also remind yourself how much they matter to you and how much you enjoy them. Are you in need of physical touch? Let your companion realize at the end of a busy day how meaningful it is to be embraced. It can seem easy, but it will get you closer together by understanding what you both need and doing it for each other.

Keep Talking

Speaking more frequently, which is something long-term partners sometimes fail to do, is one of the better ways to maintain the bond intact. So, if you're not even here, go ahead and priorities it. In any relationship, the single most significant factor is contact. Say what you like and need each other. To listen to the responses then. You might also want to go to couples' counseling or help build a bond and a means or learn how to really understand each other. Couples counseling as it is usually done using Emotionally Oriented Therapy (EFT) is now approximately 75 percent effective, suggesting couples who have gone experienced less tension in relationships. So, yes, there are things you should do, no matter how long you've been away, to feel connected again and enjoy a better relationship. When you see it, it's just about accepting a problem and making a few adjustments as a pair to maintain the flame burning.

Say 'Thank You' for Something Daily

Demonstrate to your companion how much you love and admire her or him. There are numerous little ways in which to achieve this. It may begin with something that is as plain and genuine as: "I really appreciate the coffee you create." Thanks to you.

At least once per day, give your partner your undivided attention.

Do this without staring at your Facebook stream, playing with your mobile phone or gazing at the Screen side-by-side. When your companion needs to interact with you, drop what you're doing and concentrate all your attention (and interest) on him/her by maintaining complete eye contact.

Be the first to say sorry in Any estrangement.

It's not easy to tell, "I'm sorry" if you feel wrong, so you should tell, "I want you to remember, last night, I'm sorry for my part, and I love you." No need to justify yourself. Enough has been said among you.

Ask for a Hug

Tell your girlfriend or boyfriend that you want to touch her for just a minute, understanding that she may resist, half-heartedly embrace you back, or suggest something stupid. Anyway, ask for a hug, and it might build a moment of reconnection.

Return to your real feelings of loving

Why, in the first instance, are you with your partner? Why is this guy you love? What do you want things to be like in your life together? Without telling your spouse to do or say something in return, express this with him, sharing from your heart.

Express more compassion and empathy to your Partner during Difficult times

A little compassion does go a long way, actually. You have no idea about the tension in your partner's head that replays itself. So, please want to grasp what's happening to her and bring her a little comfort.

Lighten Up and Be More Playful

Small incidents that are blown out of proportion are most disputes and misunderstandings. Hold things in perspective, find something to joke about together, and let the stress cut off with a little laughter. In keeping grudges, there is no benefit. Almost any relationship repair is achievable when you rely on love, togetherness, sincere feelings of concern, physical contact, and heartfelt gratitude for your partner. Good communication skills are necessary, but only once a healthy relationship is formed.

2.6 Emotionally Intelligent Relationship

It's shockingly clear what will make a relationship work. Successful couples are no more educated, wealthier, or spiritually astute than most. Yet they have stumbled upon a dynamic in their day-to-day lives that prevents their pessimistic thoughts and emotions towards each other from overcoming their optimistic ones (which all couples have). They support each other's interests rather than building an atmosphere of disagreement and opposition. Their slogan appears to be a supportive "Yeah, and ..." rather than "Sure, however ..." when answering a partner's inquiry. This optimistic mindset not just helps them to retain but also improves the feeling of passion, play, pleasure, excitement, and learning together that is at the core of any long-lasting relationship. They share what we term a relationship that is emotionally intelligent. As a significant indicator of the progress of a child later in adulthood, emotional intelligence has been commonly known. The sooner a kid is in contact with emotions and better prepared to communicate and get along with others, the sunnier the outlook of that person, regardless of his or her academic IQ. For spouses in a relationship, the same is true. The more emotionally aware a person is, the more often they can survive happily ever after, the more equipped they are to appreciate, honor, and appreciate each other and their relationship. Just like parents should teach emotional maturity to their children, this is also a trait that can be mastered by partners. Developing this skill will hold all parties on the winning side of the divorce chances, as plain as it sounds. One of the saddest causes a relationship fails is that when it is too late, no spouse knows its worth. The exes realize how badly they truly give up when they gave up on each other only after the harm was finished, the furniture separated, and different apartments leased. Instead of the nurturing and consideration, its merits and urgently needs, healthy relationship is so frequently taken for granted. Any persons may believe that it is not a huge deal to get separated or languish in an unhealthy relationship. They can also deem it a plain aspect of everyday existence. Although there is a lot of research now showing how devastating both divorce and an unhealthy relationship can be for anyone concerned.

2.7 Fixing Communication Issues in Your Couple

Good contact is the foundation of any and all relationships, whether with your romantic partner and otherwise, to the delight of no one. This is all well, and well, yet if you're still down the toxic path, the hard part is finding out how to address relationship difficulties. Today, "unhealthy" can imply many things, but in this situation, it applies specifically to inadequate behavioral methods that contribute to a strong disconnection between you and your significant other. What do you do while you are still in a pattern of conduct that is definitely not doing your relationship favors? And, most specifically, after harm has already been done, how can you start to heal? One significant point to remember and consider is that all problems just do not have a quick and quick answer. Each pair and relationship are distinct, and each individual has their respective needs that need to be fulfilled. In reality, psychologists have done thorough conflict-related studies and have shown that no single type of speech is actually successful across the board. In addition, they observed that, at times, even psychologist advice was considered inadequate. So, in fighting unsafe contact, the first mode of security is, that's right,' communication.' It's not because when people avoid talking, they don't know-how. "Couples will reach up to psychologists and claim," We don't know how to connect, so they're starting at the top. What have they missed in the way in the dialogue process? When have both of them started feeling safe?

Focusing on The Person and Not the Issue

Honing in on your significant other 's actions is anything but effective. It's not enticing to inform the partner they're not spending time with you; you're practically asking them they're not a really successful spouse. It's this critique that makes them want less time to spend with you. Moving to the source of this surface dilemma leads to the understanding that you really don't want more time with your partner. However, you want the other person to want to spend more time with you. You have to consider the beginning phases of your marital relationship and the aspects that drew the pair to each other originally, and what made you want to spend time together, and, most specifically, what has changed since then with your own actions that could have influenced the connection between you and your partner. In any dispute, even those including contact, self-examination should often be the first move. Place the topic on the table. We're robbing them of integrity as long as we target the human. As soon as people realize that the only thing, they can alter is themselves, they can see that they have an opportunity to progress.

Passive Aggression

This is one that's clear. In certain ways, tip-toeing or disguising the true thoughts and intentions underneath the veil of sarcasm or "passive" comments is not only dangerous but also violent. This conduct typically indicates animosity that the individual thinks he does not dare to convey openly. The behavior is also an example of the patient's resentment that he/she is over-dependent on not having satisfaction in a relationship with a person or organization. Passive violence is often also a warning that a blow-up is inevitable since bad and damaged feelings are obviously (and potentially valid) involved. A design that includes mind-reading is passive aggression. And because humans are not in the mind-reading market, this can only contribute to tragedy. Passive violence is often based on the traditional myth of conversation that you have to be cruel to be straightforward in a sentence. The question is how to tell what you expect without mentioning what you think. Without being cruel or disrespectful, yet in a way that is self-honoring of yourself, and that is good, it's crucial to figure out how to relate and speak for yourself. It is essential here to adjust your vocabulary to "share your wishes in a manner that encourages." And, as opposed to pointing the finger, still hold the attention on yourself, the emotions, your desires, your wishes. Still control the barrier and work on your side of it.

Judgment and Criticism Disguised As "Helpful Suggestions"

If the text messages are more clean, considerate, or sensitive, these little comments we put out there always mean too much more, largely because of the manner in which we express them. These 'helpful' ideas are all about power, really. When you ask your wife,' Is this what you're going to wear? 'You are disguising your decision, yes. It is important to pick your fights here. Remarking on the outfit of your girlfriend or boyfriend is possibly a moment where you should hold your thoughts and judgments to yourself. All the way, you don't approve. Yet not all of it has to be dealt for. Also, it is necessary to modify your implementation as you want to communicate your needs and requests, as stated before. A successful approach to follow is to concentrate, as opposed to the "who" or the "how," on the effect of a specific need or desire. Instead of thinking, 'You're supposed to make dishes,' or, 'The kitchen is a mess,' you might suggest, 'I really enjoy a clean kitchen,' and your companion might eventually start doing it on their own, so they realize they're going to realize that it makes you happy. In all correspondence, make sure to always have a very significant notion in mind: reverence. The esteem in every relationship is wonderful. Lack of appreciation is like oxygen deprivation. And you want the people around you, particularly those you love deeply, to be a source of oxygen. A respect-rooted expression that both couples and individuals can get into the habit of employing is, "I hear you." The meaning is very impactful, though limited in structure. People enjoy being noticed. They all need someone to bear with them. There are so much familiarity and protection in feeling that can come out of those words.

2.8 Communication Tips that Work

Relationships include some of life's biggest difficulties, whether with spouses, partners, daughters, boyfriends or even just partners. Although there are many variables relating to the performance of a relationship or long-term relationship, relational abilities may either support or impede one 's chances, or lack thereof. Would you want to change the way you connect with your significant other? Several documented and realistic tips are below that can promote good contact. Below are suggestions for common scenarios, as well as clear techniques for addressing disputes.

Use Feedback

Perhaps we're not completely conscious while we respond to our significant other or others for that matter. Maybe we're overwhelmed with everything else that's going on with our lives, or maybe we're too attentive to the intense feelings they display. It is common to find yourself in a pattern of anxiously awaiting to put a word in with a thought (defensive comment, rebuttal, etc.) in informal discussions and particularly during tense ones, when the other talks, rather than only taking it all in and then reacting afterward. Therefore, we wind up not paying complete attention to what the other person does. "Active Listening," on the other side, means having a deliberate attempt with an accessible heart and mind to calm down and listen. This is better said than achieved, of course. But the purpose is key, so you've got to start there. If you may not have the bandwidth to listen intensely and freely for some reason, perhaps you might want to table the topic, debate, etc. at another moment. Again, stated more quickly than achieved. By exchanging input, you can take active listening a step further. The typical approach to do this is to reaffirm what you have heard the other individual tell to prove your comprehension. We all know how terrific and fantastic it feels to be understood. Being seen and understood is therapeutic and may not change the paradigm in a constructive direction dramatically. You don't really have to comply with what's being expressed; however, you want to prove that to the best of your capacity, you want the other's viewpoint. It's good to be fully honest about this. You may claim, for instance, "It sounds like you are angry at me for failing to take care of or use that language." Am I correctly reading to you? Active listening is a talent and often takes practice, as too many facets of conversation. We get stronger at it when we use it more, and it gets simpler.

Edit Criticism

Create a deliberate attempt while engaging with your companion to prevent specific criticism. This means refraining, such as eye-rolling, from put-downs, threats and aggressive body language. Criticism, as we all know, makes us, among other factors, feel defensive; it greatly reduces the listening mechanism and may contribute to further accumulation of frustration and hurt feelings.

Be Gentle

If you're disturbed by something, bring it up kindly and without fault. Be careful of the sound used when addressing topics. A sound of shared respect; one that is neither defensive nor aggressive; one that goes a long way to begin a constructive conversation.

Seek First to Understand vs. Being Understood:

This one of the most effective ways which can really be utilized in all conversations, including with partners, other family members or acquaintances, as a slogan. Our mistake as human beings is always to rely on our need to be heard while in dispute. How many times have you said, "you really don't get what I'm doing."? Of course, good relationships include knowing each other, so strive to shift the concentration to give attention to knowing the other rather than stressing the own need to be understood. This will help improve the relationship dynamic and pave the way for a conversation that is more transparent and newer.

Ask Open-Ended Questions

Hmm, did you find these hypothetical queries, like, "Have you ever started communicating and listening?" or "I wonder if you're really going to carry the garbage out without telling me?" Doesn't a healthy conversation need to be initiated? Sure, at the moment, they can sound nice to say when you relieve any pent-up rage or resentment. Still, it doesn't lead to resolutions in the long run. Instead, if you have doubts, submit open-ended questions. For starters, you could say to your partner, "I could use some support to get the garbage out; do you have any thoughts about how we can do this?"

Stay Calm

Try to hold talks as calmly as possible. Take a break. Revisit when the two of you are less intensely charged if things tend to intensify. Be conscious of your self-talk; are you asking yourself something that holds you reasonably relaxed, or are you feeding the mental anxiety flames?

Use "I" statements

By utilizing "I" sentences while talking (e.g., I feel, I need, I won't), I strive to control the emotions. "Remember the" XYZ "technique:" I feel X in condition Z when you do Y. "For instance:" I feel annoyed when on Tuesdays you don't take out the garbage, the day you promised to do so.

Self-soothing

When frustrated, find ways to soothe yourself. For example, by going for a stroll or finding some time for yourself to do some breathing exercises, take a "time out." It applies to hold one 's feelings in place. When feelings are more controlled, interactions can be even more fruitful.

Accept Influence from the Other

Learn to place yourself in the shoes of your partner and be able to obey their point of view and advice. Data suggests that "relationship works to the degree that the husband can acknowledge his wife's power." Hence, be aware of the gender differences in your relationship that can encourage or hinder the capacity to affect each other.

Share Appreciations

Each individual would know in every successful relationship that they are accepted and appreciated for who they are. It may be useful to recognize what you admire in someone and mention certain aspects while talking. Studies say that when solving issues, people with good relationships create five times as many optimistic comments than derogatory ones. Sharing gratitude leads to a number of optimistic emotions because when they feel comfortable about themselves, people actually perceive it and connect more.

Chapter 3: Communicating: Insecurities and Anger

Anger can be managed by going for a stroll, doing meditation, or mindfully participating in deep relaxation. Although these are all excellent strategies, what happens when the anger in the heat of the moment is aimed at the partner? Even the most self-reflective and self-aware personality may be overcome by frustration. Your heart races, and the limbic system can seize control while you are flooded, rendering logical reasoning nearly impossible. It is crucial to recognize that indignation is always a red herring that masks emotions such as humiliation, disappointment, and hopelessness that are more insecure. Although it might not be realistic to suppress frustration at the time, the emotions within may be established. And how are you doing this? Respect your rage tale and use such words as keys to activate your main feelings behind it. Insecurity is an inner sense of being in any form challenged and/or insufficient. For one period or another, we have always felt it. But though experiencing feelings of self-doubt once in a while is very common, constant depression will undermine your life's progress and can be very detrimental to your interpersonal relationships. Chronic fear robs you of your equilibrium and keeps you from being able to participate in a secure and genuine way with your partner. The acts that come from fear are not appealing and may drive a spouse away, often asking for reassurance, jealousy, accusation, and snooping-erode confidence. While many people prefer to assume that insecurity arises from everything that their spouse has said or done, the fact is that most insecurity arises from inside ourselves.

3.1 Anger in Relationship

When you feel upset every time, pause and reflect on why you're upset. Fighting so hard in your relationship? The solution to rage is empathy. Relationship frustration and rage frequently derive from total dismay about how the partner could really have accomplished what they did. You just can't explain it. You will never have done something like that.

- He was expected to shut a company bank account for months on end, which received huge fees and which he was not really using anymore. There was still a reason, and hundreds of millions were going to be lost in the process.

- You've begged her numerous times to only play upbeat songs on radio stations in the morning. Yet she keeps turning on the classical music station morning after morning, which you told her makes you sound like you need to go back to sleep. Why does she still overlook the appeal seemingly?

- You both figured the other person had decided on Tuesday evenings to do dishes. It's almost midnight, and neither of you has done it, and all of you are secretly resenting the other. Angry, you don't want to go to bed, but this is just the back of the camel from all the other occasions that your wife didn't do the dishes that they agreed they would.

If you show any of these signals, you can understand your thoughts first and recognize the emotions you have. Then aim to locate the cause and determine why you are rendered more sensitive by external circumstances. Decide if the dilemma still matters until the companion mentions it. Get back on track, if it's not necessary, by reassuring yourself and using constructive self-talk to relax your frustration. Using either physical contact or words, strive to reconnect with your spouse. The above circumstances are indicative of the mundane resentments in existence that, when not treated with good contact, contribute to overwhelming marital issues. Resentment can escalate to rage in relationships, left untreated over time, which requires immense mental energy to remove. It's easier to treat frustration than to let it escalate out of reach. So, what is the remedy to grappling with your spouse's dissatisfaction and its potential escalation into anger? The answer is to channel the shock into consideration for the actions of your partner, strive to comprehend them, and come to the scene, hoping to consider their viewpoint. It's trite to say, but that's because it's perennial counsel. No one would need to speak much about it if it were straightforward. You invite your companion to show consolation and create a repair rather than becoming protective by dwelling on your emotions underneath the frustration. You're beginning a polite conversation regarding your emotions instead of initiating a war. You invite your companion to be on your side, too. From time to time, we all get upset with our spouses. To support you mitigate the detrimental impact of rage on you and your relationship, consider the following tips: How do we feel empathy for the people we hate, and how do we behave empathically? Some top tips are here:

Keep calm

Rage drives resentment, but the calmer you are willing to stay, the sooner the frustration of your companion subsides. Shouting in a rage at a girlfriend or boyfriend escalates her frustration, and engaging in sulking with a passive-aggressive girlfriend or boyfriend will make the problem go on indefinitely.

Show that you're listening.

People also want to feel frustrated, and they don't believe they are being treated seriously or listened to. To make sure that your companion is noticed, utilizing constructive listening strategies.

Share your feelings

If you sound frustrated too, then say so. If your partner's frustration makes you feel uncomfortable, irritated or annoyed, then address it as well. When a girlfriend or boyfriend may try to imply that her actions have any effect on you, this is particularly relevant for passive aggression.

Address anger immediately

Ask your companion what's wrong when you first start seeing the symptoms of frustration. It makes everything worse, not easier, to let an upset individual nurse her bite.

Acknowledge your partner's feelings

Saying freely, 'I can see you're upset,' and, if possible, 'I understand you're mad 'keeps your wife from believing that either by tossing her weight around or retreating into silence, she could justify how she thinks.

Show that you're listening

People also want to feel frustrated, and they don't believe they are being treated seriously or listened to. To make sure that your companion is noticed, utilizing constructive listening strategies.

Share your feelings

If you sound frustrated too, then say so. If your partner's frustration makes you feel uncomfortable, irritated or annoyed, then address it as well. When a girlfriend or boyfriend may try to imply that her actions have any effect on you, this is particularly relevant for passive aggression.

Use "I" instead of "You."

"Below is one instance of how to convey disappointment with the behavior of another spouse:" I feel resentful that the company account is still accessible. I want to ask how I can support you close the account in some way because when it is locked, I would feel very relieved and happy.

Count to Ten Before Speaking

This will make you more wisely pick your thoughts and not suggest anything you're going to regret.

Practice Active Listening

In order to validate your comprehension and share the emotions of your wife, echo what you have learned.

3.2 Aggressive Communication: Dealing with Relationship Aggression

In all of our relationships, at one point or another with a serious partner, we have gone through experiencing aggressiveness as a coping method. In reality, if this type of communication was popular in your family when you grew up, without understanding it, it may be a style of communication that you use. Narcissists and abusers prefer this coping method, but it may pop up in discussions anywhere, from the workplace to the bedroom. Emotional force is also encountered when offensive speech is utilized by one person, such that the interests of others are not really able to emerge. Others feel victimized as this arises, and relationships suffer. For the aggressors as well as the beneficiaries of the violence, relationship abuse is terrible in that sense.

Connect Physically

Hug, for one, and have intercourse. For certain people, whether the problem is in the process of being settled but is not there yet, this can include a touch of fake it before you do it. Sex actually helps to relieve frustration for most men since it is a type of communication in its own right. Although during the resolution process, you both may not be in the same emotional place, connecting physically can help. In fact, some relationship counselors suggest that they have sex at least once a day if the relationship is on a downswing. The scheduled relation could position things in a different light and help overcome frustration.

Meet on a Bridge

This can be metaphorical and practical, as well. The "understanding bridge" will need to be gapped in order to channel resentment into empathy. Integrate the notion of "we all have to be together on this bridge." Once we step onto the bridge, we just can't know what our spouse thinks. The more moves you make, the more you can see this bridge's middle "hump," where you all come together and learn the other. One suggestion is to simply travel to a bridge nearby in order to actualize this position of shared understanding. Pack a blanket and a light snack for your picnic, go to the bridge and talk about things. As well as treating life less seriously, the calming atmosphere and fresh weather will contribute to transparency. The bridge has the bonus of acting as a pleasant place to reconnect.

Engage in Daily Empathetic Actions

Empathy is not the natural emotion inherently and requires some retraining to become par for the course. By checking in with our partners on how they feel, looking them in the eye, and consistently offering the advantage of the doubt, repetitive empathy may be updated. Resentment also becomes a thing of the past as remorse becomes inherent behavior. Empathy, it points out, in relationships, is the remedy to rage. As such, feelings of empathy often drive the reduction of normal anxiety. Not only are you potentially moving to an agreement with your partner in life, but you're also both going to feel calmer. Having empathy, a normal feature of your relationship, would not only have an effect on getting on well but gradually becoming more integrated and less depressed, since it allows things simpler for you to move out of your own mind and into your partner's. As such, empathy fosters solidarity, turns narcissism into solidarity, and dismay into comprehension. Empathy forges the self-reinvention that is essential for long-lasting love.

Resisting the urge to blame

Blaming sounds fine at the time, but the results may be tragic. It does not mean that your comments can be cruel or critical, even though you feel frustrated at your partner. Here, traditional adages are right on, such as "you attract more flies with honey." Although voicing frustration or guilt will get your point across, your emotional relationship would also be eroded. Your wife is likely to get aggressive when you strike with the accusation and accuse you right back. They can even get flooded and not be able to concentrate on the topic, allowing things to intensify. Eventually, interactions like these build an interpersonal gap and the more critical and contemptuous you are, the more the relationship can chip away. It isn't easy to choose the vocabulary and feelings with caution. It requires practice, but it will restore and actually improve the relationship over time once you start using this strategy. So, the next time you feel irritated, stop worrying about why you're frustrated. Is it that you're ashamed? Worried? Scared? Frustrated? Tell your companion on what you're experiencing and what you need. A technique utilized by emotionally intelligent partners is how to understand that rage is not necessarily what you experience and how to manage the rage in your relationship.

The toll of Aggressive Communication

We may be influenced in several respects by the toll that relationship tension takes in terms of stress. It will impact our levels of tension, and our well-being and satisfaction will be impacted as well. Violent persons appear to give others discomfort and feel elevated levels of tension on their own because of the lack of meaningful interaction in their relationships when their interactions appear to be contradictory because their specific ambitions are not as frequently reached. An important technique to utilize is assertiveness in the context of hostile contact. Assertiveness is sometimes used as a synonym for good contact, but assertiveness includes voicing one's own needs and rights, while acknowledging the needs and rights of others and upholding the integrity of all parties, in comparison to aggressiveness. This leads to healthy relationships and greater happiness with life. And while relational habits are not the only form in relationships where aggressiveness will occur, those who want to shift their hostile contact behaviors to assertive ones appear to still be responsive to other changes.

Benefits of Healthy Communication

In a variety of cases, learning about communications strategies may be useful. Assertive strategies of communication will help one to draw safe boundaries with others such that we have a line of protection against any aggressiveness they display. Such safe strategies of contact can also help one from becoming unintentionally violent with others, and can also help deter confrontation. All of these significant impacts make it well worth the initiative to think about methods of assertive speech.

Assertive Communication

Being assertive involves expressing your desires while listening to the wishes of others and honoring them. It implies searching for options that are win-win rather than win-lose. It involves respectfully voicing your thoughts, describing why you feel this way, and waiting for what you desire instead of allowing someone to assume. It also implies listening well and not only seeking to hear the desires of people but also explaining to them that you hear. Among those who are used to a passive style of communicating, assertiveness can look at first feel offensive. Conversely, for those who are used to an offensive interactive form, it may sound passive. If you were not raised in a family where the standard was assertiveness and consideration for others, discovering the compromise between steamrolling over the desires of others and encouraging them to trample yours may take some preparation, but the work is well worth it. It's important to maintain being assertive in all of your relationships after you reach the equilibrium, which will eliminate tension and frustration in the future.

3.3 Your Communication Style

What do you know in the typical form of communication? Are you inclined to be violent, assertive, or passive? You can ask yourself any questions here:

- Must I check out the views of other people, or only express my own?

- Am I mad if people don't agree with me?

- Do I speak or constantly disturb people?

- Should I check-in with individuals, or should I push my own agenda to see if they are comfortable?

- Can I bring down people?

- Should I know how to make a stand for myself?

- Do I know how to disagree without being unwelcoming?

- Do I know how to satisfy my desires without compromising others' desires?

The questions above will allow you to start worrying about whether you feel happy sticking up for yourself, stepping all over someone very easily, or maybe you have reached a happy middle ground.

What Is Codependency?

Codependency applies to a dependence on a companion, acquaintance, or family member that is behavioral, social, physical, and/or spiritual. Codependency of its own is not a psychiatric condition or a behavioral illness officially classified. In general words, codependency combines features of early childhood behavior type trends, although it may often correlate with other behavioral conditions, including reactive personality disorder.

Varying Forms of Codependency

Codependency can come in all shapes and sizes and with various intensity levels. It is fundamentally attributed to weak self-concept and bad limits, like an unwillingness to provide an opinion or tell no. In all kinds of relationships, codependency may create, such as parent-child, relationship-partner, wife or husband-spouse, and even work colleague-boss.

Signs of Codependency

Codependency, as described above, relates to an imbalanced pattern of relationships where one individual takes liability for fulfilling the desires of another individual to the exclusion of considering their own interests or feelings. Thus, codependent relationships are formed around an inequity in control that encourages the desires of the taker, leaving the giver to continue to give even at the expense of himself. Certain, though not generally all, symptoms of codependency can involve the following:

- To prevent confrontation with the other guy, a feeling of "flying on eggshells."

- Feeling the need to check-in and/or seek permission to perform everyday activities for the other participant.

- Sometimes, although you have done nothing wrong, you can be the one who apologizes.

- And when they injure you, they feel bad for the other guy.

- Regularly working to alter or save depressed, dependent, or under-functioning persons whose concerns go beyond the capacity of one person to address them.

- Giving something about the other guy, even when it makes you feel bad.

- Putting the other person on a pedestal notwithstanding the reality that this role is not merited by them.

- A desire for you to like other people in order to feel positive about yourself.

- Struggling to take some time for yourself, particularly if the other individual is constantly going to have your free time.

- Feeling as though inside the relationship or you have missed a sense of yourself.

Why Codependency Is an Unhealthy Dynamic

Although everybody has loved ones and feels guilty for those loved ones, when somebody's identity is reliant on someone else, it can be dangerous. Codependency does not apply to all loving actions or thoughts, but rather to those that are dysfunctional to an extreme degree. Responsibility for interactions with others may coexist with self-responsibility. As individuals with codependency frequently develop relationships that are one-sided, emotionally damaging, and/or violent, this dynamic has often been referred to as a 'relationship addiction.' While "the giver" doesn't instantly feel this way; they probably enjoy offering their love, and depending on it; as the relationship grows, it may grow to very dangerous degrees. Another inherent difficulty is that it becomes impossible for "the giver" to get out of the relationship because they may assume as the other person depends on them too much. It is the best thing to do even though they realize it in their stomach. In comparison, "the taker" can be so focused on the other that they will still have trouble quitting a dysfunctional relationship.

How to Reduce Codependent Tendencies

Focusing on self-awareness is the first phase toward reducing codependent behaviors. This may be achieved on your own, of course, but in helping to truly unravel your codependent behavior, counseling is also quite necessary. Before their worlds tend to fall apart, those people who suffer from codependency don't pursue support. Being cautious and finding support is the right practice.

Do your utmost to do the following while you are on the journey:

- Become founder of a fan group of your own. Learn to communicate to yourself lovingly and positively, and avoid the temptation to judge yourself.

- Taking tiny moves in the relationship towards any separation. Look outside of the relationship for events and participate in new relationships. Focus on discovering and then building on the aspects that make you who you are.

- When prompted to consider or care about something else, turn your mind inward consciously. This requires practice, so along the way, be good to yourself.

- When anyone criticizes, undermines, or attempts to manipulate you, stand up for yourself. You'll discover more strength in yourself by focusing on developing your own sense of self-esteem.

- Don't be scared to tell anyone "no" when you just don't want to do anything.

- Try trying a community network or social psychotherapy if one-on-one treatment doesn't cater to you.

Codependency is a complex conduct that comes in several ways and strength ranges. It also contributes to an unstable dynamic in relationships that eventually gets worse over time as the codependent personality loses a sense of self. Self-awareness and successful behavioral redirection are crucial to eliminating codependent behaviors. Be good to yourself while you progress through years of acquired behavior.

How to Build a Relationship Based on Interdependence

Most of us, especially in our romantic relationships, respect interactions with others. In reality, we are wired for communication, and it enables us to establish relationships with our spouse and to build intimacy. Long-term relationship performance relies heavily on the nature of our romantic relationship with each other. When we think of our perfect relationships, we always think about our most significant partner as a beautiful, near, lifetime relationship. How can we create a relationship of that kind? That comfortable, secure, long-lasting relationship with someone we know has our long-lasting back? A relationship that allows us the freedom to be ourselves, that facilitates our creation and enables us to be compatible with each other? Understanding the differentiation between interdependence and codependence is one of the main factors.

What Is Interdependence?

Interdependence implies that the strength of the mutual connection they share is understood and respected by spouses while retaining a clear sense of self throughout the relational relationship. It may sound frightening or even unsafe to be reliant on another person. Growing up, we are always taught the over-inflated importance of individuality, with strong importance put on not having anyone for emotional help, to be more self-contained. As vital as maintaining a sense of control is taken to an extreme, this may potentially get in the way of us being able to communicate in a positive way with others emotionally. For those who have an exceptional sense of individuality, in a relationship while interacting with a spouse may be challenging to attain, even terrifying or not perceived as especially important in a relationship.

Interdependence Is Not Codependence

The same issue as being codependent is not interdependence. A codependent human, for their sense of self and well-being, appears to rely heavily on others. There is little opportunity for the entity to discern where they stop, and their spouse starts; there is an enmeshed sense of obligation to another person to satisfy their needs and/or to feel OK with who they are with their spouse to fulfill all of their needs.

Traits of a codependent relationship include things like:

- Poor / no personal boundaries

- People-pleasing attitudes

- Tolerance

- Unhealthy, inefficient contact

- Tampering

- Emotional relationship challenges

- Behavior management

- Blaming one another

- Strong self-esteem of either of the couples or both

- No individual agendas or purposes beyond the relationship

Codependent behaviors are not acceptable and do not allow space for spouses to be themselves, to evolve and to be independent. Either spouse or both depend strongly on the other, and the relationship for their sense of confidence, feelings of worthiness and general mental well-being are included in these dysfunctional relationships. For either or both parties, there are always emotions of remorse and embarrassment when the relationship isn't going on.

Why Interdependence Is Healthy for a Relationship

Interdependence requires a compromise between oneself and others within the family, understanding that all parties are functioning in acceptable and substantive ways to be involved in fulfilling the physical and emotional needs of each other. Partners are not intrusive from each other and do not search for emotions of worth to their partner. In times of need and the ability to make certain choices without fear of what will happen in the relationship, this allows each spouse space to retain a sense of independence, room to step towards each other.

Characteristics of an Interdependent Relationship

There are many aspects of a good, interdependent relationship. Here are a few items to search for in a non-codependent, stable relationship.

- Safe thresholds

- Successful listening operation

- Time for personal desires

- Efficient correspondence

- Take full responsibilities for acts

- Development of protection to be vulnerable to one another

- Engaging and reacting to one another

- Positive self-esteem

- Being transparent and available to one another

The relationship becomes a secure refuge and a position where the pair can be interdependent as couples feel loved and respected. In moments of need, they realize that they are not alone in the relationship, will switch comfortably towards each other and feel confident that their spouse will be there.

How to Build an Interdependent Relationship

Being mindful of who you are from the outset is the secret to creating an interdependent relationship. People sometimes search for or join into relationships merely to stop feeling lonely, without any personal examination of who they are, what they admire, and their relationship priorities. Taking time for this sort of personal contemplation encourages you to step into a new relationship with a self-awareness that is essential for an interdependent relationship to be formed. Maintaining a sense of self in your interpersonal relationships is important. In a relationship, we recommend the following strategies to retain a sense of self:

- Awareness about what you want and what appeals to you

- Not being frightened of knowing what you want

- Spending time with acquaintances and families

- Continue following your professional objectives

- Be conscious of your beliefs

- Allow time for activities and hobbies

- Do not be frightened of hearing "no."

- Do not stay little or concealed to appease others.

The trick to maintaining a safe, interdependent relationship would be to give your spouse space and the chance to do this same stuff. Starting the relationship in this way will enable both parties to build a comfortable room to learn how to move intimately towards each other without fear of sacrificing themselves or being influenced or exploited. Interdependent relationships do not leave individuals with their spouse or the relationship feeling insecure or afraid, but rather leave them feeling comfortable with their spouse. Taking time in the most meaningful relationships to focus on who you are and what you desire. In the dating phase, being aware of this will help guarantee that relationships can remain healthier and better in the long run.

3.4 How to Control Anger and Anger and Resentment in a Relationship

The manner that partners cope with frustration will also make a relationship or ruin it. Don't settle for matches shouting and doors closing. Anger is a common and usual human emotion that, even though not directed to the person to whom it is being communicated, appears to make its existence known in every relationship. Unfortunately, in our relationships with people we value the most, like our romantic partners, rage also rears its head. But in a relationship, love does not imply that feelings such as frustration are conveyed in uncontrollable ways. In every personal and romantic relationship, handling frustration and communicating the reaction to an upset spouse is a valuable ability that can foster trust and maturity. Many clinicians want their clients to reflect on how their reactivity gets in the way of who they want to be as a participant in a relationship. Very much, as a reaction to our frustration, we close down, whine to partners or attempt and manipulate our companion. Although we growing feel encouraged by these techniques at the time, they are seldom successful in the long term. Let's take a look at four basic tactics in your relationship for handling frustration and increasing maturity.

Avoid the Impulse to Cut Off

Often, they can have the need to slam a door and give them silent treatment while an individual is arguing with their significant others. Going quiet will momentarily settle you down; however, your partner's fear or frustration is likely to escalate. In the middle of the moment, this doesn't imply you have to calm down to fix a dilemma. Try asking your companion that you need more minutes to settle down so you can organize your thoughts instead of immediately zooming out of the driveway or walking away. Let them realize that it is important for you to figure out the gap and decide what the best period of time for you to reflect and return to them is. When you have missed an anniversary or skipped dinner with your partners, whether your spouse appears to give you the silent treatment, you have definitely endured some discomfort, not understanding what is going to happen. You couldn't force them to speak to you, so when they're ready, you couldn't express that you're ready to share your thinking and collaborate together. It is possible that trying to coerce or intimidate them into a swift settlement would backfire and trigger them to break even further.

Focus on Managing Yourself

We also feel obligated to satisfy and soothe them as soon as possible when someone we love is upset at us. Ultimately, however, we do not monitor the feelings, actions, or emotions of anyone; we are just concerned with controlling our own. It is much more productive to be relaxed than having to relaxed someone else, and persons who can remain focused on handling their own anxiety and responses allow the other person the room to do the same. But instead of asking, 'Calm down, please. Try to take some deep breaths to slow down the pulse rate. Similarly, if you're upset with your companion and want them to alter actions, a negative response is likely to be generated by your effort to influence them. The purpose is to express your thought, not to shame the other individual, with the intention that you will be noticed. Know, if your comments and actions illuminate the fear-response in your partner's head, it is doubtful you will be noticed. In relationships, immaturity begets immaturity too much. Sending a nasty text to your spouse when they're at work or waking them up with your complaints in the middle of the night may seem important, yet these tactics seldom do anything than worsening a disagreement.

Be Aware of Triangles

It may sound cathartic to vent to a partner, your kids, or even your therapist when you're irritated or peeved at a partner. This is also called an emotional triangle because we use a third party to handle our tension over another. It is absolutely normal to want to complain, and it is not false. Although in the original relationship, often, this "triangle" stops us from figuring out the issue, and it may leave the spouse feeling alone or perhaps making them more protective. So, the next time you're furious with your wife and tempted to pick up the call, question yourself, "Am I calling for support, or are you really waiting for someone to compromise with me?" If it's the latter, you could attempt to settle yourself before telling anyone else to do so. And while there's nothing inconsistent about your therapist's relationship tension discussion, be mindful that it's their role to remain impartial and assist you in your best thought, not to agree with you that the story's protagonist is your spouse.

Look Past the Issues

There are certain subjects as people who are prone to ignite an aggressive reaction or an agitated reaction that may contribute to confrontation. There are also subjects such as finance, politics, spirituality, sex, parenting, or family drama. It is safe to believe that possessing differing views will cause frustration and confrontation, but more frequently than our true opinions, it is our childish reactions to these subjects. So instead of getting hung up as fast as possible on dispute resolution, turn the attention back to reacting as maturely as you can possibly. It does not indicate that you are obligated to put up with a partner's harassment or volatility, or even that you have to continue in a relationship. Maturity basically looks like being determined not to let the display run absolutely over the feelings. "It feels like saying," What in this case is the better version of myself doing? And it is impossible that you can have your finest self-slamming doors or you will yell at someone you love. Remind yourself that you are 50 percent of the equation if you feel irritated by the sum of rage in your romantic relationship. If you're calmer and more stable, so you can be calmer and more stable in your relationship. Maybe your partner is going to climb to the same degree of maturity, or maybe you're going to decide the arrangement isn't right for you. You're opting not to let rage rule the stage, anyway. They are likely to meet a spouse that can do the same as one person can make the decision for themselves.

3.5 What Causes Insecurity in a Relationship?

Insecurity, at its heart, typically arises from a deep feeling of inadequacy. The prevailing overarching assumption is that the way we are, we are not enough, that we are deficient, hideous, or undeserving of affection. This feeling of "poor value" frequently falls hand and hand with either or both of these toxic habits, a stern inner critic and the assumption that only if we act in a certain manner can everyone love us. We may assume that behaving solid, enjoyable, compliant, accommodating, beautiful, hard-working, always there for everyone, whatever the collection of requirements is, is the only way to remain with our spouse. This may also sound like tricking our partners into loving us, occasionally. Perhaps not directly, yet somewhere between the lines, we can assume that they may quit the moment they learn our true colors. On the other side, we might feel helpless in front of our inner detractors, who still throw attacks at us. In our everyday self-talk, it may become so rooted that we are not really conscious about how much it has an effect on our overall self-esteem.

The Impact of Our Past on Our Current Relationships

The result of our early impressions is typical of all these beliefs. They come from the forms in which we perceived and integrated those interactions the best we could in the little tools we had in our value framework. There may be several descriptions of these early experiences:

- We formed connection styles with our primary caregivers, which we later pass to our other relationships.

- Primary messages we got from our setting that tailored deep convictions about ourselves, other individuals, and life in general

- Observing relationships surrounding us and "seeing" what we can and should not do in order not to wind up damaging.

- Hurtful events, such as being ignored by someone we cared for, overlooked, or embarrassed

While it may be tempting to fault the actions of our spouse for our insecurities, the fact is, much of the time, vulnerability actually stems from inside us in a relationship. Indeed, it will certainly shake our confidence to be in a relationship with someone who constantly evaluates much of what we do. Our self-doubt can be intensified by putting up with repeated scrutiny and occasionally receiving attention or praise from our partner. But beware, the word is to raise, not to build. It might be good to note that other individuals in a particular manner may not make us sound or act. Just our opinions and values will achieve it.

Can Insecurity Damage a Relationship?

Once in a while, it is totally natural to feel insecure. It can also be useful in limited doses at times, so it will inspire us to bring more work into our relationship. It is persistent self-doubt that may damage our mental well-being adversely and interact with our relationships. An authentic bond between spouses is one of the main elements of good romantic relationships. Authenticity is a profound bond, and authenticity allows us to be responsive to revealing our weak side. To achieve so, we need to trust that we are always perfect and deserving of affection, even with our flaws. In other terms, at least to a certain degree, we ought to feel happy with who we are. Chronic fear will stand in the way of authentic interaction with your spouse by stopping you from being yourself entirely. Constant anxiety may be emotionally draining in a relationship, stripping you of harmony and satisfaction. Obsessive doubts will turn your mind into a deeply miserable position to be, instead of loving the trip and having a nice time with the individual you value and care for.

And if you let your insecurities get out of control and affect your actions, if that's not enough of a pain, it can contribute to a series of unstable relationships with your spouse where you are still unsatisfied, and the relationship loses.

We search for Clues to Confirm Our Toxic Beliefs

Insecurity in a relationship, for instance, may also lead you to misunderstand such circumstances or to exaggerate concerns. It does not seem obvious, but as people, we are always searching for hints to validate our convictions. This offers a sense of order and power for us. We have all sorts of values, and several of them are specific and help us organize knowledge and understand it. Any of such convictions, though, maybe unhelpful and dangerous. Yet our minds may be persistent, and they still seek to validate certain convictions instead of letting go. In the sense of relationships, this implies that whether you think your companion is going to harm you, abandon you, or deceive you, there is a strong possibility that you may continue to locate signs of your suspicions, knowingly or unintentionally. This is a normal fear response-if the worst-case situation arises; you're trying to be prepared. This causes the anxiety to spike, however. Not just that, but this may also contribute to a prophecy of self-fulfillment where you continue to behave in a way that causes the same answer you tried to stop. Simply placed, where they do not appear, you can begin to encounter issues. Not only can this help fuel your insecurities, but it also adds to negative habits such as bringing down your partner, envy, allegations, and continually looking for reassurance, just to name a couple. Both those actions drive the wife apart and undermine a relationship's trust and faith.

3.6 How to Stop Feeling Insecure

Stop thinking it is all about you

You are going to have a self-centered worldview chasing boogeymen where they don't exist. Don't say it's because of you if your companion doesn't feel like heading out, because they might have had a very rough day at work that depleted their resources almost as quickly. In order to notice the meaning behind their speech, body appearance, and stance, avoid psycho-analyzing any word choice, your spouse creates to be more present at the moment. A sure-fire way to skip the argument is to obsess over veiled definitions. Don't berate your companion for being too silent or keep saying, "What do you think?" During every conversational lapse. The pattern of an anxious individual is an intense desire to fill any second of silence with needless phrases. Take the side of your wife, breathe in, breathe out, and together, embrace the quiet. Who says you can't love just living without words with each other?

Stop psyching yourself out.

Your emotions may be the best partner or worst enemy in your relationship. The consistency of your thoughts influences the quality of your relationship directly. "Have you ever found cynical thoughts like," I know someday they're going to get bored of me, "or," Why do they love me? These theories are not concerned with reality, but they have a great deal to do with anxiety. In other terms, there is no dilemma you are dealing with; you invented it. Whenever you feel uncertain about your relationship, remind yourself, "The thing that I'm concerned about occurs just in my mind." I've got absolute power of it.

Stop lugging around all that baggage.

Have you ever felt so bad in a relationship that you'd love to only wish it all away, so you never have to hear about it again? Only enter a party. Since this love thing is an unpredictable (and often rocky) journey, you'll be hard-pressed to find a guy that does not have a bit of baggage. A little baggage is totally cool, but before moving into any new relationship, you need to lighten the load. Let go of any hurtful feelings leftover that might linger and realize that your new relationship is a fresh chance to put all that behind you. The wonderful thing about life: you can start anew as many times as you need.

Stop seeing things in black and white.

If anyone faults you for something that you don't believe is your responsibility, how do you react? The survey says: get aggressive, get aggressive. Similarly, questioning your companion about a topic would most definitely lead them to become defensive, no matter how clear it might be to you. This generally leads to a knock-down, drag-out fight that is the opposite of constructive when all of you are too busy attempting to show that you are correct to settle your disagreement. Do not point the finger automatically if you have a dilemma, but instead treat your companion with sensitivity and empathy. Be relaxed with the reality that none of you is totally "correct" or "wrong." Somewhere in the center is the true answer.

Stop feeling paranoid over nothing.

Let's face it: both of them are referring to individuals of the same sex. Just because a boy and a girl are buddies (or boy and boy, or girl and girl) doesn't imply that the tale has anything to say. Stop the temptation to spoof the phone, Facebook posts, or email addresses of your girlfriend or boyfriend. While this could relax your fears momentarily when you see nothing afoul, it is still a habit that could easily become addictive, not to mention harmful when they figure out that Big Brother is watching for relationship confidence.

Stop putting off uncomfortable conversations.

While tension in the short term is painful for your relationship, it will strengthen the intensity of your relationship in the long term. Without apprehension, confronting your concerns will make you develop closer to your spouse. Never mince phrases with each other, and you can create trust so high that you can say your partner everything that is on your mind.

Stop being dependent on anyone but yourself.

Nothing short of amazing is finding someone to embrace, kiss, cuddle, make love to, and share your life with. But you need to learn to respect yourself before you march out into the sunset in pursuit of love. You should not welcome a companion into your life when it is in disarray, just like you should not welcome a guest to your house while it is a disorganized mess. Take caution if you welcome someone else to your inner-house before you. You should predict the side-effects of decreased depression and improved partner fulfillment if you let go of vulnerability.

3.7 Overcoming Your Relationship Insecurities with Communication

Fishing for compliments is your girlfriend or boyfriend. Even if they know the answer, they're telling you where you are heading. Although you've spent the whole day with them, they're badgering you for extra time. Your husband questions you frequently about spending time with a coworker who is only an acquaintance. If these incidents happen time and again, it's because the wife is nervous. Many individuals feel jealous and uncomfortable in their relationships, even though their spouse loves them unconditionally. Here's how to fend off sexual insecurities, whether you're in a reasonably young engagement or a decades-long union. When your partner is nervous, it's that something places them in a depressive condition they haven't worked with. This might be because your relationship does not fulfill their desires, or it might have to do with anything beyond your relationship, such as their own loss of self-confidence or fear of the unknown. The best thing you can do is communicate with your partner efficiently. Why does your spouse interact? What's their form of communication? You can repeatedly talk about things, but unless you really connect with your partner at their level, solving lingering problems will be challenging. The good news is, you will collaborate to resolve romantic insecurities with your partner. It can require patience, reliable contact and the ability to deepen the relationship. However, it can be accomplished. For an unstable connection with your parents, the feeling may begin early in life or may grow after getting harmed or discarded by somebody you care for. When you equate yourself favorably to other entities and evaluate yourself harshly through critical inner dialogue, insecurities are retained and founded on. Most of the uncertainty of relationships are focused on unfounded feelings and worries that you are not good enough, that without a partner, you would not be OK, that you will never meet someone better, that you are not even lovable. There are a number of items you should do as you begin to experience the sinking feeling of insecurity:

Meet Each Other's Needs

Every single person in the world has six fundamental human needs that concern them. We always aspire to be confident that we can escape suffering and achieve pleasure; we want variation in life; we want to feel important: it is necessary to communicate with others, and development and contribution enable us to find fulfillment. These needs are rated in a different way by each person, so which one is most important to your partner? Will relationship allow their desires to be fulfilled? If not, how do you adjust your habits so that you feel more valued and accepted by your partner?

Balance Your Polarity

There is one spouse with male energy in any relationship and another with female energy. These energies don't have to match with sex, but in order to find marital equilibrium, competing powers need to be involved. This concept is called polarity. Have you developed an unbalanced relationship with your partner? It may trigger insecurities to emerge if all spouses carry on male or female characteristics. Over time, look at how the tasks have shifted. How will polarity be preserved and instability banished?

Act Like You are a New Couple

The excitement is electrifying when you start dating someone different. Whenever necessary, you want to discover more about your companion and be emotionally near to them. This spark disappears with time. The sparks you first felt started to fizzle as you get more acquainted with your partner. In your routines, you get relaxed and quit striving to please. When your partner thinks like you're no longer making an attempt or that your attraction is waning, insecurities will emerge. In your relationship, put back the spark and behave as you did before you were dating. Your partner's compliment. Schedule surprising times. Post love letters to them. These little gestures will help to squash insecurities and help to feel wanted by your partner.

Create New Stories

Even in all the happiest relationships, errors are made; however, sustainable relationships will leave such mistakes in the past. What are you living with, you and your partner? No matter whether you've already struggled for money or flirtations, it's time to put those old stories behind if you're deciding to move on as a couple. Try changing your attitude instead of believing that your companion is constantly doing something that irritates you. Respect your partner for who they are, and instead of reliving past trauma, plan to build a wonderful new tale together. Insecurities, in all the most stable relationships, are likely to emerge from time to time. You can't monitor the feelings of your partner, but you can be the most compassionate, caring version imaginable of yourself.

Take stock of your value.

If you feel nervous, you are always concentrated on something about you that you feel is incomplete. Each spouse brings numerous virtues and strengths that complement the other in most well-matched relationships. In multiple forms, it is possible to be equals. In a relationship, becoming more comfortable helps you realize what you have you give the other individual. To give everything, you don't have to be wealthy, or beautiful-personality attributes are much more important to a relationship's overall quality. You might be sweet, trustworthy, humorous, compassionate, or a strong communicator. Think of the attributes you have as a human. There are qualities that are respected in a partner by most citizens. And think of the ways to make things easier for the other person: can you make them feel valued, supported, and happy? In a relationship, there are feelings everybody needs to experience, but so just don't. Instead of what you believe you need, concentrate on what you offer; this will change your outlook. If what you have to say is not accepted by the other guy, that's his or her loss.

Build your self-esteem

Data reveals that persons with greater vulnerability in relationships appear to have lower self-esteem. It is normal to want to search outside of yourself for affirmation while you are not feeling confident about who you are on the inside. Trying to feel comfortable by having your partner's acceptance, though, is a losing scenario for any relationship. You offer up all of your control while your well-being relies on someone else. This kind of burden won't want to be carried by a healthy partner, and it can push him or her away. A win-win for the relationship is feeling confident about who you are. You get to feel the feeling of well-being that comes with enjoying yourself honestly, and self-confidence is an enticing attribute that makes your girlfriend or boyfriend want to be closer to you.

It's not as challenging to construct your self-esteem as it can sound. Experience comes with developing self-confidence, so there are two measures you should take that can easily change how you feel about yourself. Learn to silence your inner judgment and exercise self-compassion, and retrain yourself instead of on those you don't want to reflect on the parts on yourself that you like.

Keep Your Independence

Two stable persons compose of a stable relationship. It may contribute to weak limits, and a diffuse understanding of your own needs to become unnecessarily enmeshed in a relationship. The secrets to sustaining a healthy equilibrium in a relationship are sustaining your sense of self-identity and taking care of your desires for personal well-being. You feel more comfortable in your life because you're not relying on your partner to fulfill all of your needs. Being an independent person that has something going on beyond the relationship often gives you a companion who is more fascinating and appealing. Places to preserve your freedom include: finding time for your own partners, passions, and activities, retaining financial independence, and setting aspirations for self-improvement that are different from your aspirations for relationships. Essentially: don't hesitate to do so.

Trust Yourself

In a relationship, feeling comfortable relies on trusting the other individual, but, most significantly, on learning to trust yourself. Trust yourself and realize that you can take care of you, no matter what the other entity does. Trust yourself and realize that when it advises you that everything is not perfect, you cannot disregard your inner voice. Trust yourself not to mask your emotions, trust yourself to guarantee that your needs are fulfilled, and trust yourself that your sense of self-identity will not be lost. Trust yourself and realize that you would be willing to quit and still be a completely functioning person if the relationship isn't working. Feeling safe is like a certainty because you trust yourself. If it feels really challenging on your own to find this kind of faith in yourself, you can need to consult with a therapist who will help you learn how to do this. It is important to note that no one is flawless, with certain baggage we all come with. Just to be in a stable, safe, and secure relationship is not important to be flawless. You can't help being a stronger, healthy version of yourself by turning your mind away from what other people say by holding the emphasis on yourself.

There are various methods and actions you may take to resolve them, based on where the self-doubts stem from.

Tame your inner self-critic

People with a powerful inner critic realize how important it is to silence the irritating voice that brings them down. The inner voice is so persistent and so compelling often that we embrace it as our truth. Because often it can be too noisy, and so rooted in our habits of thinking, the answer is not to switch it off; it's sometimes difficult. Instead, pay heed to what the voice suggests and actively speak up for yourself afterward. Treat your inner critic as you're trying to show how to be civilized and avoid shooting attacks like a misbehaving kid. In this method, you become conscious of the emotions that are self-decreasing, take a step back, and then make an active attempt to reframe them. It helps you to condemn negative views about yourself and, as a true representation of who you are, adopt a more rational approach. This sort of self-talk may sound a little bit awkward at the beginning like you're faking it. Through patience, though, it typically begins to sound less and less like a job and more and more like something real.

Make a list of your strengths

It would be beneficial to have a compilation of all your good qualities as an emergency boost to your self-esteem. In a relationship, this list reflects what you add to the table. Get imaginative and write down every good detail you might think about. Now is not the moment to be humble. Perhaps you have a pretty smile, or you're a successful kisser. You may not have a hot body for smoking, but you're supportive and making your companion feel valued. Or maybe you're not so funny, but you're trustworthy, and a fantastic cook on top of that. Nobody is pristine. But it's necessary to remember that being cherished doesn't need to be flawless. It's imperfections that make us unique. Learn to love the singularity. One crucial point to bear in mind is that the reason you deserve to be cherished is not reflected by this list. It can simply act as a reminder about how many good qualities you have, and they are simple to overlook during moments of heavy self-doubt. As a special human being, you, with all your peculiarities and perceptions and wounds and mannerisms, are lovable. Only let this soak deep. This is impossible to accept often.

Let go of conditions you imposed on yourself to deserve love.

The implicit conviction: "They can only love me if I am this or that" is what can always be found underneath intimacy insecurities and what further drives self-doubt. At some stage, you give yourself a message when you maintain this illusion that you are not really lovable at your heart, for who you really are, but that through doing some stuff and acting in certain ways, you ought to merit affection. But don't you. Our partners are selected by us, and our partners select us. You need to believe in a relationship, of course, for it to be safe. To succeed, it is important to bring effort into your relationship. It's important for your partner to do pleasant stuff, to display love and appreciation, to create trust and make them feel secure and valued. But to be a person deserving of affection, you don't need to do those things. Between the two, there is a gap. If only if we follow those standards, we feel deserving of loving, the feeling stands on a shaky field simply because we can occasionally struggle. Inescapably. Does everyone. This is why beginning to value yourself for who you are and not for what you do is crucial. To accept that you are sufficient. To know that because of you, your companion is with you (even though you're super unaware of it right now). For that, self-compassion may be extremely beneficial.

Communicate with your partner openly and effectively

In a relationship, it is important, to be honest about what you and your spouse really need and explore practical and rational approaches to support each other to satisfy them. Be mindful that this form of communication needs all parties to surrender defensiveness and stereotypes, and to be kind, truthful, and open to each other. An intimate relationship provides a secure atmosphere in which you can work and reach each other halfway to conquer insecurities. This is often not straightforward, particularly if there are everlasting difficulties and grievances in a relationship, but it can be achieved with a joint effort. It can be challenging to cope with vulnerability in a relationship, and it needs you to contend with your core values and make an active attempt to shake the habits that, for years, have shaped your thought. Even it's achievable through consistency, self-reflection, and efficient contact through your partner. And always bear in mind that this doesn't have to be a solitary war. Support and support from somebody you know will make things a lot more bearable, like a partner or a psychiatrist. Not only can learning to handle your insecurities improve the consistency of your mental well-being, but also the consistency of your romantic relationships.

Chapter 4: Infidelity, Extended Family and Couples Therapy

"Couple counseling" and "couple counseling" typically say the same thing. On a scientific basis, there is little distinction between them. The other sense in which whether the treatment is named is a legit and; in certain places, you may get a separate "therapy" credential or license to practice, which is more challenging to receive than the "counseling" credential or license to practice. Whether you name it couples therapy or couples counseling, this form of relationship with a licensed practitioner offers partners consulting services. These topics may vary from basic difficulties of understanding or serious disputes to difficulties of drug misuse and psychiatric conditions. Although counseling for partners may be a wonderful way to bond with your spouse or mend the gaps between you, without having a therapist, there are also ways to ensure sure you maintain the connection going and the relationship safe. There are several sites out there that build on couples' relationship ideas or studies. It is never too late to start adding a little more time into your relationship (or too early). Choose one or two of the practices and techniques listed below to practice with your spouse if you would like to strengthen your relationship. If you are a marital and family therapist or a psychologist for families, discuss discussing with your clients any of these practices and drills. Why are persons cheating? What will make anyone want to stray from their union and, in another person, pursue comfort? These queries have a range of solutions, all of which we will explore below. One of the first steps in repairing a relationship following an affair is knowing the common triggers of infidelity, so recognizing the root of the problem helps you to pursue a solution to it. To hear about the many explanations of why individuals lie in relationships, read on.

4.1 When to seek Help

We all realize that interpersonal bonds are hard work. Like vehicles, to maintain them working smoothly, they need daily maintenance. If there is a concern, to prevent more problems down the line, it is better to get it fixed right away. Often, we will do some of the essential maintenance and fixes. At one time or another, you might have worried about seeing a doctor. You may have reached out or told yourself that if you only wait a bit, the issue would go away. On other occasions, we need to focus on a specialist to take a look and lend us a hand, considering our best efforts. How simply and efficiently we take those measures to fix or avoid harm to our cars is fascinating. We realize that we always stop taking steps to our relationships until the problem has become even more severe. Sadly, although a large amount of injury has also been incurred, partners often attempt relationship counseling. Maladaptive marital behaviors have been ingrained, the relational connection amongst spouses has been significantly compromised, and due to unresolved past disputes, there is a high degree of distrust. The list might continue. This is not to suggest that counseling for partners will not be successful in addressing those long-standing issues.

Nevertheless, it would be a far more complex and time-consuming effort, taking a lot of devotion and commitment from all parties. Misconceptions of what counseling for partners is and its intent may often discourage spouses from finding treatment early on. You may believe that counseling for partners is mainly designed for severe conditions that impact a relationship, like infidelity or addiction. Before deciding to terminate the relationship, some might perceive it as a last-ditch attempt. Some think of counseling as a means to push their spouse to improve when they are "the question." In managing a broad spectrum of relationship difficulties, often, persons are not conscious of the advantages of pair counseling. They may not realize how critical it can be to improve the overall quality of relationships that influence individual mental wellbeing.

4.2 Times Couples Counseling Could Be the Best Option

Such obstacles are big. There are moments where you are more likely than not to catch yourself, asking, "What is it the best time to go for marital counseling? If your spouse has had an affair or your wife claims she's fallen out of love?" "Some partners question themselves if therapy can help them overcome the tension or grief they experience in their relationship, and the response is yes, unambiguously. Any psychological action can result in a sort of progress, either together or as individuals, and it is this movement that most partners desire to break through their feelings of hopeless inertia. If you're dedicated to discovering ways to save your life, it may also make you fall more intensely in love with each other by finding outside make together as a team.

After an Affair

Counseling is critical after an affair. It provides each of you with a waiting place for all the feelings that you would encounter after a breakdown of confidence has occurred: rage, guilt, resentment, frustration, sorrow, and typically more rage.

Decisions regarding the future of your relationship need to be taken, and it is necessary to find a healthy space to accept possible consequences. Although particular instruments can help drive you through this confidence-building phase, nothing can render this pain disappear. You can't completely accept that it happened and carry on, as much as everyone likes that to be so. You should set a concrete timetable for recovery in treatment, and it's good to provide a chart when you wander into this traumatic storm. When an accident arises, interpersonal counseling is indeed beneficial, since each of you wants a space to discuss, appreciate and process any of the emotions that emerge.

One Partner Claims They Fell Out of Love

Some people ask whether their partner will fall in love again, and almost as many want to know if they can bring their companion to fall in love with them again. A skilled professional will assist you in discovering the root concerns behind this relational transition and collaborate with all of you to establish a road to reconnection. There are long-standing problems for many partners, who have become so thorny with frustration that much of the emotions between them have developed into apathy. It is important to participate in discussions in these circumstances that explicitly discuss the

resentment, frustration, and guilt at the heart of the separation.

During Major Life Changes

These transitional periods are occasions that we are compelled to redefine and re-orient ourselves, such as when you have a newborn, renovate your home, leave, relocate, or suffer a big loss, which also creates a lot of conflict, uncertainty and stress that can have a detrimental effect on your relationship. At periods of transition, spouses fight further, and it brings up emotions of being out-of-control that many individuals deal with by becoming upset and turning the frustration on their partner. Any fundamental tension within you is stirred and magnified by uncertainty and the numerous decisions and distractions that occur during those periods. That's why now is a fantastic chance to find some advice and develop new techniques in conversation, such as how to reason more effectively.

Your Sex Life Starts to Suffer

If your sex life shifts unexpectedly or your relationship has a steadily diminishing degree of sexual affection, this is an indication that something has shifted, and you should find a way to speak to your partner about your desires to figure out what's triggering the disconnect. A shift in your sex life might indicate that unspoken resentments have built up and are being introduced. Apathy comes out as a lack of affection for the other individual, or as an implicit withholding as a means of revenge for unspoken or unresolved emotions of having been wronged, as rage is redirected to apathy. Of course, as a natural aspect of the aging phase, many people notice that their libido simply changes or decreases with time. However, to ensure if there is nothing more profound going on, or to work on some deeper concerns whether they occur, it is worth checking in with each other.

You or Your Partner Is Diagnosed with Illness

The dynamic in your relationship growing change from an equitable relationship to that of a patient and caretaker when you or your spouse are diagnosed with a serious illness. While in certain situations, these tasks are essential and natural, they can often contribute to feelings of disappointment, resentment, and dissatisfaction and a diminished sense of intimacy, both of which can linger even after the point of the total recovery. Chronic conditions may also impair sex life with or without physical triggers, as while they are in a caregiving role, it is incredibly hard for certain persons to feel sexual with others. Now is a safe opportunity to get advice if you and your wife face some of these roadblocks in your relationship.

4.3 Common Causes of Infidelity

Why are persons cheating? What will make anyone want to stray from their union and, in another person, pursue comfort? These queries have a range of solutions, all of which we will explore below. One of the first steps in repairing a relationship following an affair is knowing the common triggers of infidelity, so recognizing the root of the problem helps you to pursue a solution to it. To hear about the many explanations of why individuals lie in relationships, read on.

Feeling Like the Relationship Is One-Sided

The sense of imbalance in the bond is one of the key challenges that partners encounter shortly before the infidelity. There are several types of one-sided relationships: one partner feels underappreciated, the other partner feels a greater financial burden than the other, etc. As long as one person acts like he or she's carrying more weight than the other person in the relationship, it's one hand. When an entity is weighed down by the stresses of a relationship, he or she can seek relief from the companionship of another person. In other words, if your partner feels that you're not receiving enough love from him or her, he or she may search elsewhere for it. Will this render the actions justified? Oh, no. But it helps provide you with a decent starting point in the future for infidelity couples counseling.

A Lack of Communication

One of the most significant components of a good relationship is contact. Suppose you can't speak to your partner and listen to what he or she has to say. You are going to have a difficult time navigating past your relationship's daunting obstacles. For persons that steal, this is particularly true. Not being willing to communicate with their partner's secrets, stories, and emotions will cause certain individuals to open up emotionally to others. This can or may not contribute to a romantic relationship, but there is also a type of cheating that is mental cheating. It might be time to pursue the assistance of a licensed marital counselor if you are trying to move through issues in your relationship.

An Unsatisfying Sex Life

Unfortunately, since they are not happy with their sex lives at home, several individuals lie. For guys, this doesn't only matter. Because of unfulfilled sexual impulses, members

of both genders may stray from their relationships. A survey found that, relative to only 17 percent of those who were sexually fulfilled, 52 percent of people who weren't satisfied with their sex lives would be inclined to physically interact with someone they were drawn to, which implies that individuals who do not have a healthy sex life are three times as likely as those with satisfying degrees of intimacy to cheat on their spouses. Compared to 49 percent of females, 71 percent of men from the survey who had lied in the past claimed they did so out of sexual boredom. However, getting a drab sex life could put your relationship at risk of infidelity, regardless of gender. If, because of your sex life, you are worried about infidelity, you could explore the sex therapy alternative. In this situation, to maximize your relationship and reinforce your marital relations as a whole, you and your partner can consult with a sex therapist. Study better strategies to communicate with your partner and address structural conflicts that, over time, might have damaged your sex life.

An Unfulfilled Sex Drive

Before, you've already heard this excuse: "My sex drive is too high to manage for one human." This is more prevalent in males, but women may also have high sex drives. If there are still mutual intimacy concerns in your relationship, fixing such concerns will help you totally escape this source of infidelity. There could be any deeper personal concerns that he or she has to resolve if you have an involved, safe sex life, and your wife always continues to cheat on you. It is not a reason to cheat on your partner to have a strong sex appetite, but 47% of men and 17% of women who cheated in the aforementioned study listed it as one of the explanations for their affair. Speak to a couple's counselor regarding other approaches to satisfy your fantasies if you find like your new sex life is not enough to suit your needs.

Revenge for Past Infidelity

Believe it or not, since they have been cheated on previously, certain people continue to cheat on their partners. He or she could search for a revenge affair if the non-cheater is unwilling to forgive the cheater for his or her acts. This is a turbulent period, causing far more suffering than ease, yet one of the most important triggers of unfaithfulness. Contact a marital counselor who will help you conquer this challenge and move on with your life whether you and your partner are at risk of infidelity, or you are seeking to repair your relationship following an affair.

4.4 How to Deal with Infidelity

Infidelity is viewed by most committed partners as an incident that would never control them. We perceive it as a problem reserved for celebrities only. This is not the reality, sadly. About twenty-five percent of couples experience infidelity problems, with figures growing when just romantic affairs are also included. How are you coping with infidelity, then? After the betrayal, how can you move forward? How can you and your partner heal your spousal relationship? No painless relief is provided by adultery. You need time as well as a commitment toward changing in order to rebuild the trust broken by an affair.

Respond, Don't React

Emotions of disbelief, rage and sorrow are typical responses to news of the infidelity of a partner. You will need time and commitment to work through these emotions, and it's absolutely necessary to allow yourself room to absorb all your emotions and thoughts. Try repeating in your head what you are going to suggest so you can view yourself as someone who is assertive instead of being hostile. It can contribute to reckless decision-making by doing it with frustration. Learn techniques of emotional control, such as concentration, self-regulation as well as breathing for seven seconds.

Absolute Separation

The affair should be over by now. The most effective way to avoid an affair is complete isolation from the other party. It is essential to be transparent and truthful with the partner engaged in the adultery to show the other partner that they are both dedicated to the union. Taking a sudden break from your lover can prove to be a difficult task, as some kind of desire only they could fulfill. They have to be told that it is done, leaving no space for argument. Safe relationship recuperation is difficult without complete separation.

Accept Your Part

The dishonest partner must admit and accept complete blame for what transpired. They need to be fully transparent and forthcoming and provide an explanation for other questions. It will add to debates on what has gone wrong and what should be improved. It's better, though, for the cheating partner to stop providing any single aspect of their unfaithfulness since this sometimes contributes to wounded expectations rather than healing. It is only necessary to disclose as much of the details for your partner to understand why and what has happened. Confidence would not recover immediately, so it is a healthy starting point to take accountability.

Commitment and Changes

The cheating partner has to develop different habits in order to contribute to repairing the union. Constant reassurance is the most essential improvement. You can supply your partner with reassurances regarding your devotion to them regularly, and then you can follow through with action. Providing your partner to judge you is important: providing them complete access to phone and everything that you might have held more confidential throughout the affair. Such activities will help rebuild the broken trust.

Identifying the Needs

Everyone has basic emotional requirements that offer the greatest degree of pleasure to them as they are fulfilled. Emotions of anger and unhappiness arise because they are not fulfilled. This is when, instead of expressing these needs to their partner, the deceiving may look beyond the union to fulfil these needs. Both partners should communicate their desires to one another and work together to meet them. Active listening is one approach of established efficiency-a deliberate attempt to understand the entire meaning being conveyed. Active listening means validating the thoughts of each other when they are articulated as well as paying attention to grasp rather than respond. This strategy of collaboration will enable them to truly grasp the desires of each.

Heal by giving Space

The early time is always extremely difficult when discovering an affair. It needs full dedication from all parties to discover the path to rehabilitation and healing. There isn't a duration fixed for the issue to be resolved, but most partners endure the affair. They are actually happier and more devoted to each other. Time alone is not going to repair the relationship-both partners need relentless commitment.

4.5 Using Communication to Prevent Infidelity

What sparks affairs? What more people care about is the absence of affection and unsatisfactory sex. Yet bad contact is a bigger source of infidelity, actually. In one poll, for 68 percent of men and 75 percent of women, inadequate contact lead to an affair. Far less relevant was sex. In a relationship, if contact is so critical, it should be a goal. To maintain the relationship safe and to avoid infidelity, here are several ways to use contact.

Why communication is so important

Communication is like a glue that ensures a stable relationship or relationship. There are also aspects in which it makes you stay together:

- Dealing more effectively with concerns

- Make better options

- Have fewer claims

- Establish closer ties and greater faith

Communication may have a significant influence on a relationship's progress. But really, what does it mean?

Types of communication to prevent infidelity

There's more to conversation than simply chatting. In a relationship, it's general integrity, transparency and togetherness. Contact requires stuff like:

- Spending time and sharing encounters together with each other

- Real and mental closeness and ease

- Life sharing, choices and parenting together

What is your relationship like? Make sure you're not neglecting any of these places if you want to better protect against infidelity.

Prioritize communication to prevent infidelity

There is a greater possibility for a stable relationship to last. In your relationship, make an attempt to maintain contact accessibly. This will help develop connections and improve your relationship with your girlfriend or boyfriend. You would have a stronger base to focus on as rocky times arrive. One of the largest factors of infidelity may be minimized by effective contact.

4.6 Couples Therapy and Extended Family

There are a handful of challenges that typically emerge from the range of "how do you really see things that way," and the beliefs and standards around the families of each other are perhaps the most common. There's an illusion that you naturally both inherit and know the relatives of your partner while you are a couple. How challenging it can actually get to know each other's families is often taken for granted. And because of this, it's a dilemma when couples quickly throw their hands up and give up because they don't appreciate the effort involved.

In-laws can provide an opening to meet and experience closeness in family

We always speak about the burden of in-laws; however, many people will, of course, have wonderful relationships with the parents of their spouse. There's a good thing to being a child of two communities. An extended family may be a chance to get a different way of understanding closeness and family. The bond with our own parents determines very much of our understanding of relationships. And equally, it may be powerful to see interactions handled differently. It teaches us that there are several different avenues to look at our relationship.

Merging two family cultures

As stated before, in relation to the counseling of partners, the role of relationship is to combine two cultures in order to establish their own. We do not mean merely merging South Asian and Western European cultures, to be sure, although that is definitely necessary. We also say the combination of the way the Smith's do it with the way the Jenkins do it. We also draw decisions on how we can handle stuff. But combining two families and two separate cultures also implies tangling with different standards of transparency, family visits, money, caring for older parents, etc. In fact, multiple individuals have very simply different understandings about how the family is described. It can also be remembered that there are further problems in a culture where conventional gender stereotypes are less proscribed. If everybody believes in a given society that a woman will provide for the parents of her spouse or that the financial decisions will be taken by the spouse, there are fewer decisions to be made. They ought to draw up their own laws and society as partners realize they don't want to subscribe to these laws. This is exciting, sure, but a lot tougher as well.

Be more curious and enthusiastic about your partner's family

About every counseling for partners includes certain features of a class of spiritual theory. First, ideals must be tested, so to speak, what are your beliefs, how can you describe what family is, what kinds of duties do you have to each other's lives, who gets to make choices, etc. For families from very diverse cultures, it's easiest to see this, but it does not always require certain strong cultural discrepancies to be present for extreme differences in beliefs. In your relationship and about the family and desires of your wife, it is necessary to be curious. Even if they assume, they already know the answers, we are major believers in couples asking each other questions. "Look if you're shocked," I'm trying to plead, when a patient asks, "I already know what he or she is thinking ...."

Issues of privacy with families

Privacy is a major issue concerning each other's family. What kinds of problems are "close" to the relationship and not to be shared, therefore? Privacy is deemed the standard in most Western culture-when a pair argues. For example, there is always a perception that this cannot be shared. Therefore, privacy is particularly burdened when we consider our understanding of things to be an inalienable privilege. "Of course, I figured you wouldn't inform your sister about our battle" resides right next to "How could you imagine that" don't inform anybody "implied that I wouldn't tell my sister." Both can sound irrational to a respective spouse in a rough moment, and both can come up against feelings of protection and confidence. We look at why privacy is crucial in couples counseling and what limits should be placed on it, but also look at the expenditures, such as maintaining the relationship separate and unwilling to use outside support. A wonderful resource may be one another's parents, siblings or other members of the family. It is astonishing how much it can change your understanding of each other. For example, the thoughts of a spouse regarding privacy are not mad or evil, but rather an expression of distinct beliefs. To navigate the gaps, you are always left. However, the tenor of the discussion will shift.

Couples therapy helps by including another person in the relationship.

It will help to have another adult partner in the relationship, the psychiatrist of the pair while coping with issues about the family perceptions and beliefs of each other. What can't be done by the two of you, the three of you can. Your aim should be to bring the pair to where they feel less isolated and will get anyone in the discussion who may not have the same preferences (like family members) as the other participants. The three of you can work out how to develop different avenues that will help you get unstuck in the relationship itself and in your relationship with each other's families.

Chapter 5: Arguments and Conflicts

Conflict in a relationship may be a major cause of tension. If the tension in your relationship is unresolved, it causes uncertainty that will adversely impact both you and your partner's well-being and well-being. Here are some ways you can be physically and emotionally impaired by disagreements in a relationship, along with several suggestions about how to handle this and cope. The conflict between relationships is a conflict between entities (for example, families, partners). There might be anything like a divergence in view, knowledge, taste, viewpoint, appearance or values at the center of the dispute. Disagreement is normally serious enough to affect any part of the relationship, such as conversation, and defines disagreement from merely holding a separate viewpoint. It is not only committed couples who may encounter contradictory relationships, but families can still disagree. Family disagreement may trigger a considerable amount of tension, whether it's a direct discussion about lunch or some underlying sense of dissatisfaction that stays unspoken. There may not be a lack of affection amongst stakeholders, instead a lacking in confidence in the handling of confrontation. Although it is always perceived as a rough and painful, tension is not necessarily a negative thing in a relationship. While it is stable and constructive, relational tension offers participants an ability to think about how the environment is viewed and perceived by others. It can contribute in building imaginative solutions to issues and help individuals evolve. However, it may be detrimental to anyone concerned where confrontation is not constructive or good. Sustained and unresolved conflict still can build stress at home and at work, may erode relationship intensity and confidence, and may also because individuals feel physically ill or painful.

5.1 Conflicts in Relationship

Conflict is practically impossible in a relationship. Conflict is not an issue in itself; how it is treated, though, will bind persons together or break them apart. A cause of frustration and distance, or a springboard to a better relationship and a happy future, maybe weak communication abilities, conflicts, and misunderstandings. Keep these ideas on good negotiation skills in mind every time you're grappling with confrontation, and you will produce a more optimistic impact.

Conflict and its Effect on Health

Research shows that disagreements in relationships will adversely alter your health. As an example, over a period of two years, more than 650 adults analyzed and found that "healthy unpleasant exchanges in social situations" (in plain English, repeated or sustained conflict) were substantially correlated with minimum level of self-rated fitness, greater functional restrictions, and a greater variety of health issues. These results involve

many health variables, but it seems that stress will damage the immune system, one important takeaway. Conflict contact will render you more vulnerable to contagious conditions such as a cold. Few persons often suffer persistent stress-related

discomforts, such as migraine and discomfort in the back or stomach.

Conflict has adverse Physically effects

Science might really back up those songs about the agony of a broken heart. Extreme and unexpected mental distress or physical distress triggers Usually, "broken-heart syndrome" produces intense chest discomfort and distress, close to what anyone might experience should they had the heart-attack. Social isolation study has found that the discomfort of isolation and social-rejection is handled by the similar part of the brain which manages actual discomfort, which can be a reason as to why getting rejected by your beloved may literally harm. The disorder may also be triggered by the tension between spouses or at work. You may acquire an enhanced vulnerability towards physical pain. You can even become insensitive to it when you are constantly subjected to stress and conflict in a relationship.

Acknowledge Conflict or it Can Hurt You

Conflicts are unavoidable. Relationships where persons "never argue" aren't really as content as they claim to be. It may potentially be toxic when the rage is hidden or not acknowledged by partners or your family members. Research has shown that both spouses appeared to die younger in relationships where one spouse habitually resisted rage. Recognizing and successfully managing disagreement, maybe a road to better communication between two parties, moving them together.

Conflict getting out of Hand

Being aware that there are dangers to the unresolved dispute which could make you believe you have a right to express your frustration in whatever way you find available to anyone you want. That is not exactly the best way, though, to handle confrontation.

5.2 Conflict Resolution and Mistakes that can be Avoided

Conventional wisdom and studies suggest effective communication will deepen relationships, raise trust, morale, and support. The reverse is also true: bad contact will break relations, create tension, distrust and even disdain! Since confrontation is essentially unavoidable in relationships and not inherently a sign of difficulty, if you develop the expertise and skills to approach tension in a safe manner, you will minimize a large amount of tension and improve your relationships at the same time. Here are several instances of negative and even damaging behaviors and modes of speech that, in a relationship, may escalate the conflict.

Avoiding Conflict Altogether

Rather than expressing building frustrations in a cool, polite fashion, before they're about to burst, certain people simply don't say something to their partner, and just blurt it out in a furious, hurtful tone. This appears to be the least painful path, definitely preventing conflict, but typically brings more discomfort to all sides as tensions increase, resentments fester and inevitably results in a much larger dispute. Addressing and settling disputes is far safer. This diplomatic skill of assertiveness will assist you in expressing something in a manner that you are more likely to be understood, without disrespecting the other individual.

Being Defensive

Instead of answering the grievances of a spouse with an impartial mind and a desire to consider the point of view of the other party, aggressive persons steadfastly reject all misconduct and try diligently to stop looking at the potential of contributing to an issue. Denying accountability can appear to relieve tension in the short term, but when couples don't feel listened to and unresolved issues and begin to develop, it causes long-term problems.

Overgeneralizing

When something occurs that they don't like, by drawing wide generalizations, others blow things out of proportion. "You constantly," and, "You rarely," as in, "You every time come home at midnight," or, "You never do anything I want to do!" Pause and worry about whether or not this is really real. Even to take the conversation off-topic and to stir up further negativity, don't bring up previous disputes. It stands in the face of serious conflict settlement and boosts the degree of disagreement. We are often not conscious of the forms in which the imagination will blow something out of proportion.

Being Right

Deciding that there is a "right" way to look at things and a "false" way to look at things is detrimental, and that your way of viewing things is accurate. Don't insist that your companion see it the same way, even if they have a contrary viewpoint, don't view it as a personal assault. Seek a consensus or consent to differ, and note that a "right" or a "wrong" is not necessarily there and that all points of view may be correct.

Psychoanalyzing" / Mind-Reading

Instead of thinking for the thoughts and emotions of their companion, individuals often conclude that they "reflect" what their spouses think and feel based entirely on inaccurate impressions of their behavior, and therefore presume that it is harmful. For e.g., determining a late partner doesn't care enough to be on schedule, or that out of passive-aggressiveness, a sleepy spouse, rejects intimacy. This causes misunderstandings and animosity. You should bear in mind that we all come from a particular viewpoint, trying hard to presume nothing, just listening to the other individual and making them clarify where they come from.

Forgetting to Listen

Instead of actually listening and wanting to comprehend their partner, several people talk, raise their eyes, planning what to say next. This prohibits you from understanding their point of view, which stops you from getting to see your partner. Do not neglect the value of truly listening to the other person and empathizing with him. It's important to be mindful of these listening skills.

Playing the Blame Game

Through judging and punishing the other party for the circumstance, several persons struggle with confrontation. "Alternatively, attempt to view confrontation as an opportunity to assess the problem critically, consider the interests of all sides and come up with a compromise that benefits you all. They perceive acknowledging some vulnerability of their side as a deterioration of their integrity and deny it at all costs, and sometimes tend to blame them for being" at fault.

Trying to "Win" the Argument

When people have centered on the statement "won," the relationship fails. Mutual recognition and agreeing to a compromise or settlement that satisfies the interests of both can be the point of a relationship negotiation. You're centered on the wrong path if you're making an argument about how unfair the other individual is, discounting their emotions, and remaining trapped on your point of view.

Making Character Attacks

Often individuals take from a spouse some negative behavior and turn it up into a personality defect. For example, if your boyfriend leaves his socks lying about, looks at it as a character defect and labels him "inconsiderate and lazy," or labels her "needy," "controlling," or "too challenging," if a woman wishes to resolve a relationship issue. This produces detrimental impressions on both sides. Even if you don't like the actions, remember to value the guy.

Stonewalling

Often people actively stonewall or fail to speak or listen to their partner when one partner tries to address disturbing concerns in the relationship. This reflects disdain and, in some cases, even disgust, thus encouraging the inherent tension to evolve at the same time. Stonewalling does little but generates relationships with unpleasant emotions and hurt. Listening and addressing stuff in a polite way is even easier.

5.3 Tips for Conflict Resolution

Although confrontation is a fact of life and connected to other individuals, the relationships do not always have to be jeopardized. It also improves the relationship as you understand how to identify tension and function through it in a safe manner. The key is to develop your dispute solving skills and constantly enhance them. Learning how to be an active listener and practicing assertive communication are only a few qualities that will help you navigate interpersonal problems in a positive way by being able to understand and recognize your emotions and communicate them clearly. If you and your wife have a marital dispute, there are few unique tips that will make things simpler for you to work through it together. Ok, here's how.

Stay Focused

Even while coping with current issues, it's easy to dig up past apparently connected disputes. It seems necessary to fix all that concerns you at once to have it all addressed whilst you are still struggling with one disagreement. Unfortunately, this also clouds the dilemma and allows it less possible to achieve common consensus and a remedy to the present problem, thus making the whole debate more challenging and often frustrating. Try to not dig up hurting problems in the past. Keep concentrated on the moment, your thoughts, empathy and seeking a remedy for each other. Practicing meditation on mindfulness will enable you in all aspects of your life to strive to be more aware.

Listen Attentively

Sometimes people believe they are listening, but when the other person is talking, they are just worrying about what they are going to discuss next. Remember to remember that the next time you do something, you're in dispute. Good contact really goes in both directions. Although it may be challenging, strive to genuinely listen to your partner and what they are doing. And don't disturb it. Do not get protective. Only listen to them and think back on what they mean, because they realize that you've understood it. Then you will have a greater view of them, and they will be more able to hear what you have to say.

Try to Fit in Their Shoes

All of us mainly want to be noticed and acknowledged in a confrontation. To bring the other individual to see it our way, we speak a ton from our viewpoint. This is reasonable, but too much emphasis will backfire on our own ability to be understood above all else. If we do it more often, ironically, there's no emphasis on the view point of the other guy, and no one feels heard. Learn to always understand the other side. Consequently, maybe you can describe you more. When people feel understood, they are more inclined to respond.

Respond Empathetically towards Criticism

It's quick to believe like they're mistaken and be more defensive anytime someone criticizes you. While feedback is painful to bear and sometimes misunderstood or distorted by the emotions of the other individual, it is necessary to listen and respond to the distress of the other individual and react with respect towards their viewpoint. Look at what is real about what they mean, too; at you, it can be useful knowledge.

Own When it's Your fault

Realize that accepting your mistakes is a personal responsibility, not a vulnerability. Good contact requires knowing that you're mistaken. Suppose all of you bear the blame in a dispute (which is generally the case), search at what is yours and confess to it. This diffuses the case, provides a successful precedent, and reflects maturity. The other party is often always motivated to react in response, bringing you all closer to shared awareness.

Include "I" in your Messages

It's less accusatory, sparks less defensiveness, and lets the other party consider your point of view instead of feeling threatened, instead of saying, "You fucked up here," introduce sentences with "I,". Make it about your emotions and what you are experiencing, such as, "I feel upset when this occurs."

Settle with fair Compromise

Look for options that satisfy the interests of all, instead of seeking to "win" the case. This emphasis is far more productive than one party having what they would prefer at the detriment of the other, either by compromise or through a new imaginative approach that offers each of you what you prefer. A good relationship means seeking a settlement in which all parties will be satisfied.

Introduce Time-Out

Tempers get hot occasionally, and it's just so hard to maintain a conversation without it being a disagreement or a battle. It's safe to stop for a minute from the conversation before you all cool down if you sense anyone f you or both of you are beginning to get rather upset to be productive or exhibiting any destructive behavioral habits. This can include taking a stroll and calming down in half an hour to return to the discussion, "sleeping on it" so that as long as you return to the talk, you can process what you feel a bit better or whatever seems like the right match between the two of you. Effective contact also requires understanding when and how to take a rest.

Keep at It

It is also a safe thing to take a break and then come back for the debate. When each of you handles the issue with a positive mindset, shared interest, and a desire to consider the viewpoint of the other or pursue a compromise, you will make strides in the aim of a dispute resolution.

Don't Shy away from asking for Assistance

If either of you have difficulty being polite during the confrontation, or if you have attempted to settle tension with your spouse, and the problem just doesn't seem to change, you might profit from a couple of therapy sessions. Counseling for spouses can assist with these issues and will teach you some techniques to solve potential conflicts. You will also behaviorally profit from traveling solo if your companion doesn't want to participate.

Bonus Tips for handling conflict

- Note that shared respect and seeking a compromise that pleases all sides should be the focus of good negotiation skills, not 'winning' the debate or 'being correct.'

- Bear in mind even though you don't like their acts, it's necessary to be respectful and considerate of the other party.

- Here are a number of traditional types of conflict mediation that are ineffective. Are you doing any of them? If so, throughout your life, your weak communication skills may trigger additional stress.

- Say you have it under control? Take our quiz on assertiveness and find out.

- For partners, you may even use multiple applications.

5.4 Conflict Resolution Skills for Healthy Relationships

A predictable feature of nearly all relationships is confrontation. It may also be a serious cause of tension. So, like most disagreements, it's necessary to find a compromise. This sounds like a simple assertion; however, often individuals hide their resentment, or either move along to get along. Some assume that they are generating one through resolving an issue, and merely remain silent when offended. This is not, alas, a safe long-term approach. An unresolved dispute may contribute to frustration in the relationship and further unresolved disputes. In reality, perhaps, more importantly, unresolved conflict may have a detrimental effect on your well-being and longevity. Sadly, settling disputes can also be tricky. Improperly treated, efforts at conflict mediation will potentially make the problem worse. Researcher John Gottman and his students, for instance, researched the way spouses battle, and may potentially determine which spouses will go on to divorce by studying or ignoring their dispute solving ability. Couples who continually attack the behavior of their spouse, or break down through conflicts instead of proactively, politely working through the dispute, should lookout. For those who did not grow up in a

family where flawless dispute solving abilities were modeled on a regular basis (and how many of us were, let's face it?), here are few tips to make conflict negotiation more

Get in Touch with Your Feelings

Just you, understanding how you feel and why you feel that way, are an integral aspect of dispute resolution. It might appear like your emotions should be clear to you now, but this is not always the case. You feel frustrated or resentful sometimes, but you do not know why. On some occasions, you worry like the other party doesn't respect what they're expected to do. However, you don't know precisely what you expect from them, or even whether it's fair. Journaling can be an efficient way to stay in contact with your own desires, feelings, and aspirations so that you can express them to the other individual more efficiently. This method often brings up some fairly severe concerns, and psychotherapy may be effective.

Hone Your Listening Skills

How well we communicate is at least as critical as how well we articulate ourselves when it comes to successful dispute resolution. If we want to come to a compromise, it is important to consider the viewpoint of the other individual, rather than only our own. In reality, it can also go a long way towards settling a dispute by only making the other party feel noticed and understood. Effective communication often encourages you to close the difference between the two of you, and realize where the disconnection occurs, etc. Unfortunately, active listening is an ability that not everyone understands because it is normal for people to assume that they are listening when they are simply formulating their next answer in their brains, thinking about themselves how incorrect the other individual is, or doing something rather than attempting about consider the view of the other individual. In your own viewpoint, it is often normal to be so stubborn and rigid that you simply do not consider the point of view of the other person.

Practice Assertive Communication

It is also an essential part of dispute mediation to express the thoughts and needs explicitly. As you already know, it may be like pouring gasoline on a fire to tell the wrong thing, and making a confrontation worse. The key thing to note is to clarify, without being offensive or placing the other party on the defensive, what is on your mind in a manner that is transparent and assertive.

Seek a Solution

When you consider the viewpoint of the other party and recognize yours, it's time to find a remedy to the dispute, a remedy in which you will all survive. Often a clear and clear resolution arises up because both sides accept the viewpoint of the other individual. A clear apology will help wonders in situations when the dispute was centered on a misunderstanding or a lack of perspective into the other's point of view, and an accessible dialogue will get us closer together.

Other times, you have to put a bit more effort. You have a few choices in situations where there is a disagreement over a topic, and both parties do not approve: occasionally you may choose to differ, most times you may reach a compromise or common ground, and in some instances, the one who feels more strongly about a topic can have their way, hoping that the next time they can confess. It's important to come to an agreeable position to attempt to hammer out stuff in a manner that is fair to all concerned.

Know When It's Not Working

Because of the burden of a person's unresolved dispute, it is often best to bring any space into the relationship or break links altogether. On the other hand, when coping with troublesome family members, introducing a few limits and respecting the weaknesses of the other party in the relationship may offer some stability. Letting go can be a great source of stress relief in relations that are unsupportive or marked by unresolved tension. Only whether a relationship can be changed or can be let go should you determine?

Strategies for working through Arguments

Success in relationships is not based on whether or not partners dispute. That's how people reason. In any interpersonal relationship, disagreements are inevitable and they will lead to development when they are treated with an approach to resolution, instead of being a growing reason for stress. Any explanations of how to address argumentative discussion productively are given below. It is necessary to be careful as we are aware that with any form of approach for choosing a single one is optimal for the particular scenario. It is easy to preach than practice.

Validate and then Apologize

Make your companion feel that, by validating them, you have a good idea of their viewpoint. It can sound stupid, but if possible, don't hesitate to take accountability for what you did and apologies.

Change the topic of conversation in a subtle yet sensitive manner

If you're in a debate that doesn't go somewhere, shift the discussion center. In a soft, thoughtful way, it is necessary that your partner should not feel disregarded. This strategy would fit well on certain claims. But it could be appropriate, with extremely volatile subjects, to arrange a period to review what is relevant to all participants.

Use humor

When utilized at the correct moment, levity can help a lot. Hop to lighten it up with some laughter or foolish action if you feel you are caught in a loop of misery. Often, this will snap a pair from a rage trance. It's crucial to be considerate in how and where to utilize humor, like other tactics, such that your better half doesn't feel like their issues are being humiliated.

5.5 Never Compare your Relationships

"I wish that my husband will be like my ex. He was so much more compassionate! "It will never make me feel bored in bed if my wife were like ..."

Your relationship could be on the quick track to failure if these feelings sound familiar!

There is an ancient phrase that says, "Comparison is the thief of joy." For decades, and for a good cause, this sentence has been around. The moment you decide to equate your companion to another relationship is the moment you want to be disappointed. Your partner isn't your ex, and they're not the husband or wife of your partner. They are special, with their own range of perceptions and convictions. Avoid contrasting everyone else to your partner and start looking at their good attributes and respecting them for who they are. Here are a few explanations of why your weakness would be the temptation to compare.

It isn't fair

Consider your two favorite foods. Maybe you prefer pizza, and you enjoy roasted broccoli as well. Broccoli and pizza are two very distinct classes of ingredients, but you enjoy each of them. About your present girlfriend or boyfriend, the same may be assumed. They might not have the same traits as your last partner did, but that doesn't imply you can value them any less. In separate respects, they're both fantastic!

Comparing your partner is not fair

If your only aim is to alter them, you cannot get serious about anyone.

It will make you feel bitter.

If all you can think of about how your wife did X, Y, and Z with you and you hope your current partner was like that, you have a serious issue! Herc's a good bit of dating advice with partners. For a cause, you and your ex aren't together. "As the old saying says," It's called a divorce because it's broken. "Loving your girlfriend or boyfriend to be like an ex (or a wife from someone else's relationship) can make you feel bitter for the affection your wife displays. You'll just be left feeling sad in the end. Instead of accepting them as they are, you will tend to hate your partner for who they are not, which is seriously hazardous terrain to be in,

It sets unrealistic expectations

It may be tempting to get caught up in the past under the right conditions and begin contrasting your partner to somebody you cherished before, but be advised that doing so can mean the end of your happy relationship. The moment you start contrasting your engagement to the life of your buddy or ex is the same moment, you begin to be disappointed. About why? And it creates the partner's unreasonable standards. We just wish we could take the best bits of any relationship we have ever been in and shape them into the right partner, but that's science from Frankenstein! Such unreasonable aspirations

would just wind up leaving both of you sad, so it's better to absolutely stop them.

It makes your spouse feel worthless

"When your partner came to you and asked," I wish you were more like my ex.? Do you picture the marital counseling you might need? "In the bedroom, they seemed more playful" or "The boyfriend/girlfriend or boyfriend of my buddy seemed so much more romantic than you do. Can't you be like them anymore? The chances are that your companion will feel insignificant because unappreciated, and that's precisely how your partner would behave when you start contrasting them with others. And if your companion began to pick on characteristics from someone else, since no two relationships are the same, that will not be a duplicate of your past experience. You should not anticipate your new partner's love to sound like someone else's, for every relationship is a beautiful experience of its own.

You're missing out on the good

The longer you want to look for your spouse's demise, the more unhappy you are going to feel in your relationship. Instead of dwelling on something you would want to improve in your relationship, look at the attractive aspects of your partner. They may not be as caring as your ex-girlfriend or boyfriend, but what are they doing that is making you wild? Create a note of how they display love and write down what they do that makes you happy or the characteristics you think impressive that they have. Having a visible checklist will help inform you in the first place of all the great reasons why you fell in love with your partner.

It shows you Don't Respect your Partner

A fantastic relationship is all about respect. It indicates you're giving your spouse honor or confidence. You are mindful of their limits and feel appreciation for their good attributes. You're not expressing love for what an amazing person they are when you equate your partner to anyone else. Comparisons may be a bit shallow, and instead of contemplating the wonderful facets of your relationship, such as what successful partners you are or how much you connect, you just care about what your partner will do about you.

What steps to take if you can't stop comparing

A marital therapist can help if you are trapped in a loop of spousal similarities. Your psychologist will assist you in getting to the core of what makes you experience the pressure to keep your relationship to the level of everyone else. A marital therapist will also provide partners sound relationship guidance on creating trust and improving their ability to connect and overcome disputes.

5.6 Improve Your Communication Style

Learning to talk assertively helps you to value the wishes and privileges of others, including your own, and establish relationship limits while making people feel valued at the same time. These measures will assist you in your relationship to build this positive leadership style and alleviate tension in your life in the process.

Be Factual About What You Don't Like

Keep to accurate explanations of what they've accomplished while confronting others regarding conduct you'd like to see improved, rather than utilizing derogatory marks or phrases that express judgments.

Don't Judge or Exaggerate

Being factual on what you don't like about someone's actions is an effective start, without overdramatizing or criticizing. The same refers to explaining the consequences of their actions. Do not exaggerate, mark, or judge; define only that.

Use "I" Messages

It comes across like criticism or an insult when you start a sentence with "You ..." and places individuals on the defensive. If you start with "I," the emphasis is more on how you feel and how their actions influence you. It also indicates greater ownership and less guilt for the reactions. This tends to mitigate the other person's defensiveness, model the action of accepting accountability and drive the two of you towards substantive progress.

Put It All Together

This formula offers a straightforward, non-attacking, more responsible means of letting people know how their actions affect you when using for objective facts, rather than assumptions or marks. For instance: "I feel assaulted when you scream."

List behavior, results, and feelings

A more sophisticated version of this formula requires again, placed into factual words, the consequences of their actions. Try to consider win-win: See if you can find a solution or a way to fulfill the expectations with all of you. Maybe a new meeting spot will enable them to stay on schedule in the case of the always-late partner. Or you can only opt to make reservations at periods when your life is more flexible, and you won't be too overwhelmed by their lateness.

5.7 Intimidation: A Common Relationship Issue

Intimidation is a powerful strategy that partners use to intimidate, monitor and even punish one another. To threaten, according to the definition, is to avoid obedience. Interestingly enough, couples claim that others that are transparent and hostile are not the actions they are frightened by. Actually, couples are terrified by the implicit secret actions that make them feel bad and liable for the unhappiness of their partner. When one participant reacts by being unhappy during a discussion between a pair, it is nearly difficult for both participants not to yield. The talk is over; the threatening partner wins. In fact, though, both individuals have endured tragic losses. The definition goes on to claim that threatening "implies reducing to a condition where the heart is weakened. This undoubtedly describes the partner's mental state that has been intimidated into submission. Similarly, the expense of threatening others is also greater. The person who is aggressive must lose his sovereignty, in which his confidence is weakened, and bravery is destroyed.

Childish Communicating

Look out for tones you could speak from a parental role. Childish communications include deferring and sending, finding guidance or description, becoming subservient or servile, pursuing acceptance and/or critique. None of the mentioned characteristics have a role in an egalitarian relationship in the relationships of two separate people. And the way you talk to one another, and be mindful of yourself and mindful of your partner.

Communication with Non-verbal Cues

This type of communication relates to how the expression of one's body leads to the communicating phase of thoughts and responses. Non-verbal contact is not a mode of expression that is harmful. By comparison, attempting to interpret what the other partner is doing or saying may be really useful. What someone says often does not correlate with what he or she expresses non-verbally. Sometimes, these mixed signals create misunderstandings. You need to consider all signals first, even though you disagree. Then you have to determine which are more relevant and reflect effectively on what someone might be thinking or experiencing. A non-verbal message is always more genuine. Some of these conflicting signals are transmitted in relationships between couples. A spouse will say "Yu are my love" during the day, then act indifferently and without affection. A partner can announce involvement and concern for his / her partner, but the partner simply interrupts or becomes overwhelmed if the partner speaks for himself. Pay heed to what it means in your acts. Let your speech and words fit. In other terms, how you connect verbally as well as non-verbally, be real.

Chapter 6: Setting Boundaries and Respecting Your Partner

It isn't often convenient to establish limits. The process itself can also be overwhelming, particularly for those who are not used to it. Letting people know where your criteria and boundaries are. When individuals are accustomed to relationship limits that are at a certain level, if you want to alter the limits for them, they will put up a battle, and individuals (like children) also attempt to challenge boundaries between each other. This can all be overwhelming, particularly when the toll of confrontation on levels of stress is taken into consideration. The end result, though, may be well worth it: relationships that require higher degrees of mutual integrity that satisfy the needs of all interested parties, and that produce far less tension for all.

6.1 Setting Boundaries

In establishing limits, the first move is to obtain an awareness of where your own personal limits lay. How happy are you with individuals coming close to you and bringing with you those freedoms? Sometimes, the impression you get that your parameters have been broken is the first hint. Since multiple entities have differing limits, you might not be disturbed by anything that affects others and vice versa. Therefore, it is necessary to clarify to everyone where the thresholds of ease and pain reside such that persons with varying limitations can be able to prevent exceeding theirs. The following are general recommendations to help you become more conscious of your own personal limits.

Assertive Communication

By and tension from confrontation and providing you with social encouragement while experiencing tough times, assertive communication will improve your relationships. A respectful yet assertive "no" to unnecessary demands from others will help you to prevent your schedule from being overrun and encourage peace in your life. An appreciation of assertive speech will also help you cope more effectively with demanding families, colleagues, and co-workers, reducing drama and tension. Ultimately, assertive communication helps you to establish the required lines in relationships that enable you to fulfill your needs without alienating others and without having frustration and frustration sneak in. This allows you in relationships to get everything you need whilst helping your loved ones to fulfill their needs too. Although many individuals associate assertive contact with tension and disagreement, assertiveness genuinely enables individuals to be stronger. Assertive engagement requires preparation. Many people confuse assertiveness for aggressiveness, but the balanced middle ground of aggressiveness and passivity is simply assertiveness. Aggressiveness contributes to emotions of harm and bonds that are broken. Passivity, and often sometimes lashing out in the process, contributes to tension and anger.

6.2 Signs You Need to Work on Boundaries

- You sound resentful of individuals demanding so many of you because that always appears to happen.

- You catch yourself saying yes to something you'd prefer not to do, mostly to keep someone from being offended or frustrated.

- You notice yourself becoming resentful that for someone, you do better than they do for you.

- You prefer to carry other individuals at the length of an arm because you risk having others come too near and crushing you.

- You feel that much of what you do is about other persons, and they might not really enjoy it too much.

- In an attempt to satisfy them, the guilt that you get from failing people is higher than the burden of doing stuff that worries or hurts you.

Questions to Ask Yourself

When you look at concrete decisions that you can make, rather than your thoughts in general, there are certain things you can ask yourself that may help you determine whether or not a limit needs to be established. In various cases, the following questions will help you explain the limits and work through potential ones:

- Would you like to say yes or no, so no one is disappointed?

- Looking at all the advantages and costs (both real and intangible) in this case, is it worth the effort to answer, yes?

- Will you feel safe approaching someone else with the same request?

- If you say no, if people are angry with you, do you really believe as they come from a polite, fair place? (And, if not, maybe it's time to consider establishing those limits?)

- Is this the pattern you want to set? (And, if not, where is the right spot to draw the line?)

- Think of someone you think has really strong standards, the kind you want to imitate. In this case, how do you think they will respond?

You should tell whether you just want to establish a barrier after you've decided how you feel. In an ideal scenario, we just need to convey the detail to others until we are conscious of where our specific comfort zones lay, and a relational limit is established. However, boundary-setting requires any bargaining very much in the actual world, and it doesn't all go smoothly.

People have limitations of their own that do not align, and for their own purposes, they do press for greater distance orcloseness. Changing the limits of the status quo may often lead us to react, often in ways that render us uncomfortable, by attempting to improve the previous or current limits. Setting limits in this way may be a war. When choosing when to specifically place your limits in individual cases, the questions to ask yourself while determining when your specific limitations are different from the questions which ask yourself because they take into consideration realistic considerations such as the 'fee' of setting limits. They will help you to be transparent about concerns such as shame (should you feel guilty? And is it worth motivating? Because you can go on with the least amount of tension. Here are some questions to ask yourself:

- What's fair here?

- Would your approach always seem to be rational if you were in the other person's position?

- Have you agreed to this, or is this an obligation that is put on you by the other person?

- Is there a particular approach here that would be more win-win?

- Can the process of modifying or setting a limit cause more tension than it can remove in the long run?

- Do you get a sensation as you visualize the outcome a year from now that this will be a stronger option than what you have now?

- If you set a limit and you believe like the other party is irrational in combating the barrier, then you are happy to let the relationship go rather than be upset by the inconsistency of the limit?

It is necessary to remember that when you have to deal with the repercussions of your actions, you would definitely weigh your own emotions more highly than the emotions of others. You are indeed one of the repercussions of your decisions and will have to suffer. Ultimately, for guidelines, we all have our own comfort levels, but these issues offer fodder for thinking. Working on boundary-setting techniques will bring some good outcomes in your life after you've established where to put the boundaries.

6.3 Demonstrate Respect

The backbone of any good relationship is respect. So, what is reverence exactly? Respect suggests that you realize that your spouse is an actual person and not just a way to get what you want. It indicates because you realize that you have different perspectives and perspectives than your spouse, and that's all right. Just because you don't hurt your spouse physically or call them names doesn't mean you treat your partner with dignity. There has to be a healthy amount of respect on the part of both parties to maintain a great relationship.

Demonstrate trust

In every relationship, including non-romantic ones, confidence is important. But it means a lot more than trusting that your partner won't cheat on you, and having faith isn't just as effective as communicating that through your acts, you trust your partner. By not messaging or continuously calling your girlfriend or boyfriend, you will show trust. Instead, text them once or call them. Leave a note that you're worried about them, and you're expecting to learn from them shortly. This illustrates that while they may, you expect them to reach out to you and that you realize your spouse appreciates your efforts. This could go without saying, but without permission, don't go through your partner's phone or personal products. Speak to them about it if you get a peculiar impression if they are attempting to conceal something from you. When there is nothing going on, there is no reason to stir up drama.

Be mindful of how you communicate.

Communication is the most essential and one of the toughest aspects of a relationship. That's because, for your partner, being open and truthful implies being open and honest about yourself. Don't ask a mind reader to be your partner. It's important to speak honestly about what is troubling you if you're angry. And don't be accusatory. Using "I" sentences, such as "if you change our plans at the last minute, I feel very neglected and unimportant," or "I feel irritated when you keep telling me to hang out while you realize I need to prepare."

When someone values my time, I always appreciate it. Your opinions are still true. Don't feel guilty about how you feel. Often, everybody disputes, and that's completely OK. Don't leave or close down contact as you do. At the very least, inform your spouse that before you speak, you are frustrated and need some time to calm down and organize your feelings. They don't sound like you're disappearing from them this way or dismissing their emotions. Validate the sentiments of your companion by doing statements such as, "I understand why you feel that way," or "I appreciate what you mean." Communication does, though, go beyond language. By carrying the cologne, they want, sharing a playlist with them, or giving them roses, you will convince your companion that you care.

Be reliable and accountable

Trust is an enormous part of a relationship, so how do you trust someone if they regularly change plans or, worse yet, lie? Follow along as you make arrangements. Don't say yes to a dinner that you don't realize you're going to be able to go to. Be responsible instead. When you and your wife are making preparations, have a schedule and update it. Don't tell that you're going to call and still don't. Set up an alert on your computer instead. Being dependable honors the patience and mental energies of your spouse. It can be frustrating to make plans regularly alter, after all. There would, of course, be periods where you have no choice but to postpone, there is a family emergency, you are hospitalized, you have overlooked a major exam on which you have to prepare. You shouldn't feel bad about these requirements (or be asked to feel guilty!). But if you prove that you are mindful of the impact that such acts (whether they are in your influence or not) have on your spouse, that will help a lot. Apologize, try to reschedule, then when you are clear, make sure you check in with them.

Encourage time apart

You may feel so nervous when you're in a new relationship that you want to spend all the time with the girlfriend or boyfriend. That's completely natural. However, the other essential relationships of your life can be simple to overlook, such as with your family and partners. No one entity will take care of both the social and emotional needs, no matter how amazing they are. And everyone wants a break every once in a while, from their significant other. Spending time alone or with other people ensures you will still begin to evolve as people. You should also add to your relationship fresh concepts and events, keep things fun and entertaining. It also offers you both an opportunity to speak to your partners and relatives about your relationship. Wouldn't you want to show off a little bit of their new love?

Appreciate your differences

For their ideas or desires, don't blame your partner. With others, you should differ and yet share their view. The variations are part of what makes relationships amazing! Even if you should not eventually change your mind, your companion will make you view the world from a different viewpoint. By attending to their football game or art exhibition, you will exhibition your companion you value them, even though you might never normally step foot in a baseball stadium or art gallery. Respect the limitations of your partner, particularly though they are different from yours. Do not harass them if your spouse doesn't want to kiss in public, or have sex, or lie to their partners. This is oppressive and harmful, probably.

Get to know yourself.

You're not really getting to know some person in a relationship. You get well acquainted with yourself. Being in a relationship will help you find out from the people you're near to what you want and need. What are you going to agree on? Which characteristics complement your own? What are the main beliefs on which you can't compromise? You may not notice if your companion isn't the way you are about R&B music, but you can't stand if they're rude to your pet. As a person and as a spouse, get to know yourself. Knowing yourself lets you connect, and it would certainly be noticed by your partner. Knowing your specific limitations makes it far simpler to know where those thresholds have been reached and when a relationship can be broken. In this region, couples who are less conscious and accomplished may notice that their lack of esteem brings their relationship down to a lower degree of well-being. There are several easy measures that can be done to avoid and substitute habitual habits that are insensitive for more responsible forms of responding to them. But not inherently simple, the following measures will increase the

level of confidence in your relationship so that it can expand and thrive:

- Listen attentively to the wishes, preferences, and fears of your partner.

- Show that you are mindful of the wants, interests and interests of your spouse by focusing on what you learn about your spouse.

- If your spouse is blunt with demands, respond to what he or she asks and behave in a timely manner on such demands. Leave no place for procrastination; turn up, honestly.

- Say terms of gratitude, appreciation, and respect for not just what your partner does, but who your partner is.

- Be sure to always taunt playfully and not harm with harsh barbs by utilizing humor to enliven the relationship.

- Only create similarities to others for the intent of bringing focus to the abilities and skills of your partner.

- The data is accessible that only you are privileged to know; never break confidentiality.

- To iron out disagreements during disputes, compete wisely with your spouse.

- Be alert not to venture beyond the limits of critique when bringing a case.

- Replace biting sarcasm for vocabulary that is soft.

- Talk to your companion individually instead of voicing your concerns with others.

- Banning all expressions of disdain, like eye-rolling.

- Omit from the contact irritated and irritable sounds.

- Be supportive and supportive as your companion makes unskilled decisions by suggesting something like, "We all make mistakes and should benefit from them."

- "Validate the offers of your significant other with supportive terms, such as," You are full of positive thoughts.

- Make space for the design of your companion. There are several strategies to get work finished.

- Assure your spouse that many perspectives have space.

- Help the decisions your spouse creates if you can.

- Acknowledge some amount of financial commitment to the family costs that your wife makes.

- Recognize the non-partnerrial, relational level of how much your spouse cares to you and your families.

- Apologize as soon as possible should you make an unqualified decision.

- Take accountability for the reasons your companion is hurt by you. Get busy learning about your breakdowns, such that your relationship does not have to be affected.

- When your companion makes bad mistakes, be swift to offer forgiveness.

- Tell your companion that she or he is proud of you.

- Declare in front of everyone your admiration for your partner.

Be sure to reassure your spouse that you are overjoyed with the relationship you are co-creating and that you are grateful to have a spouse who is deserving of your love. These suggestions are only a starting kit; you should surely come up with any of your own stunning suggestions. You have a reason to believe that you will quickly find yourself in a more enhanced relationship if you obey these basic guidelines. Don't take our word for it. Look at what you think and see your own perspective. And make sure that you respect the phase as best as you can. It boils down to listening and being nice to your spouse. You could be in an unhealthy relationship if your wife tries to know where you are all the time, constantly suspects you of lying or stealing, puts you down, calls you names, or is physically violent in some way. Abusive relationships, rather than consideration, are based on dominance and influence. Per year, they take a significant toll on millions of people's lives. Be conscious of it.

6.4 Mindfulness-Based Relationship Enhancement

This method consists on a series of strategies utilized to further reinforce coping skills linked to conflict within the relationship of partners who are still happy in each other's company each other instead of being in distress. In their lifespan, both partners will experience life difficulties and stressors. It is beneficial for partners to learn skills that facilitate working with each other in a constructive manner, healthy coping mechanisms as these stressful times of life occur. It is where the strengthening in mindfulness-based relationships falls in. The overall aim of improving mindfulness-based relationships is to master the art of being present at the moment, to embrace any obstacles you encounter personally and with your partner, and to take the time to adapt and make choices to prevent the detrimental influence of rushed decisions taken in haste and impulsively.

Mindfulness

It is instrumental to stop for a minute to think a little about the idea of mindfulness before we try to appreciate mindfulness-based relationship enhancement. Mindfulness relates to the current moment. It focuses on the state of being concentrated attention and consciousness. It also requires being informed about the encounter, being accessible and welcoming it. You should not respond instantly to thoughts and your feelings that move around in your mind while you are behaving mindfully. You behave instead as a non-judgmental spectator who, without responding automatically, discusses and accepts emotions.

How is mindfulness serving you?

You start discovering how to manage all or multiple aspects present in your life as you begin to practice mindfulness. Mindfulness able you to treat life and the entire universe in a more conscious way, rather than becoming a wasted talent. It makes all aspects more fun in life; it allows you to see more objectively, allows you to stay "under the present," and improves the capacity to interact with difficult situations.

Mindfulness-based improvement of relationships is essentially the application to the intimacy field of mindfulness strategies. MBRE, so that it is extended to partners, has the exact same function as MBSR. MBRE advises couples how to minimize and diffuse disputes and problems instead of encouraging differences to intensify, which may arise when a couple react out of haste and hurry or in frustration or fear.

Components

MBRE consist on following basic area:

Mindfulness

Which consists on learning to be both positive and the opposite in the moment without evaluating any experiences. This implies feeling but not contributing to present-moment perception.

Acceptance

It is about learning to appreciate interactions as raw experience, culminating in greater understanding and consideration towards oneself and your spouse.

Relaxation

It is about learning to create a reaction to relaxation that helps to control tension and enhance well-being as well as the clarity and capacity to maintain that state of being relaxed.

Self-broadening: Creating for all a more holistic sense of confidence, attachment, and affection.

In your relationship, emotions and opinions, MBRE often means providing insight and looking into your habits of experiences. It may be because each of you has slipped into detrimental forms of thought or dealing with one another which should be changed. In a relationship, what's the value of mindfulness? Being careful as a person, in general, implies not being wrapped up with all the small issues of life. It also includes not being distracted by the bigger problems of life. It also means being agile and non-judgmental, acknowledging distinctions, being less receptive, and becoming more impartial. Both of these attributes can support you well, in confronting everything together and just sharing time with each other.

Advantages

These are some of the proven advantages of improving relationships focused on mindfulness? Scientific research to confirm the beneficial benefits of using mindfulness in strengthening relationships is strong and increasing.

Some of the key MBRE advantages include:

- Increased trust in relationships

- Increased recognition of one's partner

- Enhanced human well-being

- Reduced tension in relationships

- Improved solutions to mental tension

- Enhancements of relationship perceptions

- Other types of adaptive contact

- Enhanced reaction to relaxation

- Calming psychological tension

Improving a mindfulness-based relationship may include utilizing different techniques. These techniques make it easier for you to be more in touch with your partner, your family and yourself, and to improve your tolerance, and see conflicts that emerge as obstacles to be solved rather than risks to your relationship. Think of what comes in your mind as a defining moment in your relationship; you find yourself angry. The probability is that either or both you and your partner have become angry and confrontational instead of working and knowing. Although tension will contribute to confrontation and unpleasant feelings, you can feel kindness and appreciation at the moment while you practice mindfulness, which can enhance your relationship outcomes.

Mindfulness-based relationship development has a lengthy tradition of established advantages to assist you as a pair to create a better and more robust basis. MBRE is very effective and useful to brace you for anything life throws at you as well as struggles you will inevitably encounter, such as raising children, work loss, financial problems, sickness, etc., while you are still in a stable and optimistic relationship. Although these activities will throw off several partners, you would be best equipped to connect with each other. MBRE helps you to do that in an adaptive manner and be conscious of the way your specific conduct impacts your relationship and other aspects in your life.

6.5 Master the Art of Negotiation to Improve Communication

Sometimes, tension is fueled by miscommunication. When couples start to quarrel, rather than fixing the dilemma, there's always an emphasis on winning the war. Without judgment, you have to listen to each other's thoughts and views. Keep the tone and vocabulary calm and accessible when answering questions. It becomes harder to settle on a target when you've defined the problem. There are a variety of ways in which the problems can be overcome.

- **Compromise:** Both sides agree to stand off slightly. But this may be a minimal approach to address a dilemma, with compromises being rendered by all parties, but maybe without an overall answer being reached.

- **Collaboration:** By partnering together to discover a different path to create a compromise that works for both parties, partners reflect on how to meet that target.

- **Exchange deal:** One spouse corresponds with the desires of the other, but in exchange, makes a proposal that he or she believes is of equal worth.

6.6 How Can You Feel Comfortable around Your Partner?

It is not abnormal to feel a little insecure and apprehensive at the beginning of a new relationship, but as time passes and things become more intense, it's incredibly necessary to learn how to feel secure in your relationship, so you won't let your satisfaction be compromised by anxiety. These anxieties that were present at the outset of their relationship would vanish for certain individuals, and they don't even have to make any attempts to do it; it just happens easily. Others, particularly those who have been injured previously, can find it a little challenging to let their guard down. Maybe they don't want to feel that agony again. That's why they prefer to build walls around themselves to help defend themselves. In the long run, the future of your relationship and, indeed, your satisfaction can be significantly impaired by this action. That's why this uneasiness should be tackled because while you're with your partner, you'll be able to feel more comfortable. Here are a couple of good and effective tips about how to hold in mind how to stay secure in your relationship so that you cannot let anxiety impact your happiness:

Get to know your partner very well.

Trying to get to know your partner really well is one of the most crucial activities you can learn to understand how to be secure in your relationship. Find out all about their preferences, their passions, to see how many things you have in common. When you are with them, you may become more relaxed, and you will let your guard down without fearing that they will harm you.

Talk to them

If you are distressed by something, clearly speak to them and explain the issue. Tell them what's troubling you or what's been on your mind for quite a while, and you'll see that your fears are unreasonable indeed. By talking more frequently, the easiest way to address every conflict in your relationship is. When you're with your best half, you'll feel more secure afterward and more relaxed.

Share your Secrets

We're not suggesting that right from the outset; you can confess them your deepest darkest secrets, just make sure you reveal those things about you, details that no one does, so they can get to understand you better and see you for what you actually are, not for what you seem to be. We all wear all sorts of different masks around strangers, so as they are one of the most valuable people in your life, your spouse should recognize you exactly as you are.

Improve Yourself

In your relationship, another way to be relaxed is by constantly striving to strengthen yourself. For starters, if you need to shed a few pounds or tone up a few muscles, start exercising or go to the gym. The main thing is to take the initiative and attempt to enhance those stuff that annoys you regarding yourself because you'll still be secure in your relationship until you feel comfortable with yourself.

Love Yourself

You can first be happy with yourself in order to be comfortable with your relationship. Learn to love and embrace yourself for all your strengths, and particularly for your weaknesses, just the way you are. We all make mistakes. No one is flawless. The essential thing is to focus on changing certain areas that you don't like too well and not be so harsh on yourself because you are always fine in your partner's view.

Remind Yourself that you both are together for a Reason

Start telling yourself that they want you for a cause, whether you have any questions, fears or insecurities. They're with you, and they just can't resist those facets of you. So even though your grin or the way you pose in pictures doesn't like you, they genuinely find you attractive and are really happy to be with you. Only pay more attention to what they mean, and you can notice they want exactly certain stuff that often makes you feel uncomfortable.

Have Patience

Always have ample time, so overnight, a relationship can't get intense. Give yourself ample time to understand more about each other and get to know each other better. Spend time together to see if there are any shared concerns you have. Don't hurry; take your time, because one of the most beautiful periods of a committed relationship is the beginning of a relationship. And though you might find it a little challenging to be with the boy or girl you often love, though you fix certain challenges that torment you, and if you have enough courage, you'll learn in time how not to let anxiety impact your happiness. In your relationship, do you feel comfortable? When have you done this? If you have any other ideas about your relationship about how to be comfortable? Do say, do say.

6.7 Why some Relationship Fails

Most of us want to find the "perfect" partner and to settle down, and most of us want such a relationship to last. The bulk of intimate and romantic relationships, at the same moment, result in a breakup. What are some of the big causes? Every pair is alike, of course. The further two persons spend their life together, the more probable it is that dynamic variables are involved. The collection of explanations below is not supposed to be exhaustive. Any of the more popular and destructive reasons behind relationship breakup are clearly described by them. Although breaking up is the last thing partners like to worry about, the unfortunate fact is that it happens a lot. In reality, as many as 50 percent of relationships in the United States inevitably result in divorce, according to recent research from the American Psychological Association. But how can you know if it is going to withstand your relationship? Ok, including your bedroom behaviors, the way you debate, and how much you talk, there are surefire statistical comments. Also, the manner in which you handle your day-to-day discussions will shed light on the durability of your relationship.

Trust Issues

One of the most damaging infections to the long-term survival of a pair is failure or loss of faith. Without confidence, two of the main anchors of a stable relationship are lost by a relationship: stability and protection. Factors such as envy, possessiveness, irrational rigidity, mental infidelity, physical/sexual infidelity, relational gameplay, lack of loyalty and loyalty, lack of emotional help, lack of financial stability, and lack of mutually compatible interests can cause confidence problems. If you think confidence in your relationship is a big concern (or was in your previous relationship), investigate whether the loss of faith is focused on a history of proof (such as substantially broken promises) or mostly emotional feelings (such as jealousy without proof). Evaluate frankly if the lack of confidence is focused on unjustified suspicions.

Holding your partner to unrealistic standards

Your companion is usually trying the best they can, but occasionally they can slip up and make mistakes, like any person. And when these slip-ups are treated by a loving spouse as an adult, an unsupportive one would treat their partner like they should be fine 100% of the time, resulting in resentment from both sides. There is a temptation to want to improve them when your individual doesn't step up to anything they didn't really sign up for, not realizing that your own actions play a major role. It provides for excuses as to why they are the issue when dwelling on the ex.

Different Expectations

It's not convenient for a person to walk together on a long trip. At the outset of a relationship, the factors that sometimes pull two persons towards one another-physical desire, romantic excitement, mutual preferences, personality links, socio-economic backgrounds-also become less essential as the pressures and demands of daily life sets in. Over time, the relationship aspirations of a pair will vary, since they tend to see their respective life goals as "what I want," rather than "what we want." Any of the explanations for a couple's relationship difference include: Does "Mister / Miss Correct" or "Mister / Miss Correct Now" see you as your partner? In other terms, how serious is your wife about staying with you in a stable long-term relationship? For your spouse, what about you?

Differences in Priorities

In respect to the relationship, the spouse has various goals and desires. The important-other relationship (and family) is the primary life core of gravity for others. In terms of its value, little else gets near. A romantic engagement, also a dedicated one, is just one aspect of life for some. There are also other facets of existence that should justifiably take greater importance from their point of view.

Moving Through Life at Different Speeds

This can be a cause of relationship separation where one participant is learning and increasing at a fast rate, while the other is stagnating. A spouse progressing steadily in her profession and culture will be one indication of this, although her significant other remains are stagnating at home. The pair's technical and social spheres continue to diverge, and the pair themselves quickly distinguish. They have developed apart, mentally, culturally, and socially.

Compatibility Issues

A broad area deserving of maximum volumes of its own is relational consistency. In my novels, relationship stability is addressed from many viewpoints in-depth, including attraction stability, personality type compatibility, and attachment style compatibility.

Withdrawing during Arguments

It has been shown that couples who acknowledged that they sometimes withdraw through disputes recorded becoming more depressed and apathetic about the overall relationship. For relationships, removal is the most troublesome. It is a defensive technique that individuals employ when they fear they are being targeted, and there is a clear correlation between withdrawal and lower overall satisfaction with the relationship.

Communication Issues

It's a huge one here. Several reports have listed contact (or a lack of it) as one of the key factors for the care of spouses, as well as one of the main reasons for break-up and divorce. After two decades of research, a credible authority on couple studies believe that the single strongest indicator of divorce is whether either or both spouses display disrespect in the relationship. Contempt, the reverse of reverence, is sometimes conveyed by derogatory judgment, critique, or sarcasm toward an individual's importance. This is recognized in communication studies as being "tough on the person, soft on the problem." Contemptuous contact acts kill a romantic relationship's well-being and intimacy.

Narcissism

Narcissistic personality disorder has been defined as "a psychiatric disorder in which persons have a distorted perception of their own worth and an intense desire for respect." Narcissism is also distinguished by a loss of real relationship intimacy. Signs of narcissism can involve (and are not limited to) complicated arrogance, grandiose self-image, rights, conceit, breaches of standards, false beauty, the Don Juan phenomenon, deception, irresponsibility, infringement of laws, excessive selfishness, negative feelings, and disrespect for others. Significantly, findings suggest that elevated narcissism is associated with infidelity vulnerability.

Relational Abuse

Relational abuse is described as the persistent mistreatment of a person for the purpose of this topic. The above are instances of emotional violence: verbal, social, physical, and/or sexual assault. Manipulation of anatomy. Narcissism through Pathology. Passive-aggressivity pathological. Excessive domination and influence.

Life Habit Abuse

Life behavior abuses are attributes that, while the spouse may or may not be personally concerned, such as a hidden gambling problem, may potentially have a negative effect on the relationship. Examples of neglect of living behaviors include opioid use. Addiction to alcohol. Addiction to gambling. Sexual dependence.

Grown Apart, Boredom, Staleness, Rut

There are a few elements to remember whether either of the four words written above resonates with your relationship experience: Whether you have been in a relationship for two years or less, and you and your wife have developed apart, it may be attributed to a lack of commitment, different expectations, loss of compatibility, or the normal trial phase and partner-finding error. If you are in a long-term relationship, it is likely that the responsibilities of life (such as education, employment, and particularly child-rearing) have interfered with the bond and shared the evolution of spouses.

A typical example is the "empty nest" phenomenon when parents unexpectedly seem like outsiders to each other after all the kids have grown up and left home, have not relied on each other for too many years.

Money Issues

The longer a person has remained in a stable relationship together, the higher the risk of financial incompatibility. Differences over money were one of the top causes of the relationship breakup, according to a study. In order to provide financial challenges, a pair may not need to be together either. Money concerns and conflicts, including and not limited to faith, protection, security, strength, influence, and survival, tap into some of our deeper psychological needs and fears.

Workbook: Building Emotional Intimacy and re-connecting in your Relationships

Relationship, Love and Communications skills in relationship

For couples who want to do new things and strengthen their bond, there are even more opportunities out there. Below are a few of the finest workbooks that will help couples strengthen their relationship. Tell yourself these questions and explore them with your partner. Rediscover one another at the beginning of your relationship and revisit the burning love and intimacy you shared.

Questions to Ask

- Do you hope you had the perfect words to inform your partner before you said anything that will leave the two of you isolated and much more distant?

- Do you ever fail to describe yourself and your emotions by not finding the right words to convey to your partner?

- Do you catch yourself with your partner in the midst of a dispute, and you realize you have no idea how or why it happened and what to do about it?

- Do you wish to be more profoundly understood by your partner?

- Would you prefer it if your partner could speak to you freely and frankly and not withhold?

- Do you hope that you could "Avoid Walking On Eggshells" and know that they will understand empathetically; without fear of what they would think of you. What might they think and how they'll respond?

- Would you want your companion to come through with what they claimed they were planning to do?

If any of it is true, we've got the solution for you.

Relationship Activities

In order to develop a stable relationship and ward-off divorce and breakup, there is no "best" behavior for partners because each partner is different and will have different best practices. In case of certain couples, it might be joining together in a common sport, such as riding a horse, playing a beloved game, or playing guitar together. In case of some people, when gazing at the stars, drinking morning coffee, or lying still in bed in quiet, it could be the prolonged chats they sometimes have. The only thing that counts is the activity, no matter what it is:

- What do you both like to do together?

- What is it that both of you can perform together and regularly?

- What is something fun for both of you?

- What is something which helps you to engage with your partner in a pleasant and thoughtful manner?

These requirements do not significantly list down the universe of activities, because that's how it is supposed to be. Some medication that works for one pair for a successful relationship may not fit for another pair. Each relationship has its distinction and should definitely be recognized as the special bond. The following activities could be a good place to start if you're confused about what activity maybe even better for both of you.

Icebreakers

The ancient faithful effort to get citizens together; icebreakers. We are sure that you recall these from your academic years, training, or any context where strangers are expected to work together or communicate with each other. You're not going to have to crack the silence and awkwardness with a stranger this time; you're going to get to understand your partner more.

Continue to ask these questions such as:

- Tell me about yourself, something weird.

- Tell me which is your most favorite ice-cream.

- Say me a beautifully random story from adolescence.

For this activity, don't be shy to get tips or feedback from real icebreakers. Whenever you have the urge to be more open to your partner, being able to explore any fun new stuff, use this exercise.

Truth Game

While you may love to watch Game of Throne with your beloved, we are sorry; the four parameters do not satisfy that. You can, though, function in a different kind of game: The Truth Game. Now, what you will ask questions about your partner and honestly answer questions about your partner. The main target of this is to better your relationship so that the root of the issue will vary from the smallest topics (favorite TV show) to the toughest (greatest insecurity or wish).

For instance, you can ask questions, such as:

- What is your worst fear?

- If, right now, you can be somewhere on the planet, where will you be?

- What is a fond recollection of your adolescence that is dear to you?

- What kind of music is really appealing?

- Who or what inspires you?

This easy game will encourage both of you to exchange personal and meaningful information with each other, strengthen your relationship and build up the foundation of your relationship.

Sharing Music

Music sharing is a profound activity that is intimate and highly meaningful, one that has the capacity to be challenging to communicate with others. Although revealing something so intimate with your partner can make you be overwhelmed and insecure, it is a gamble that might pay off well. A stronger and more integrated relationship with your spouse could be the payoff, something which is certainly worth taking a risk. Taking the time to reflect on your favorite songs and listen to them. Select songs that align with your unique tale of life highlight, your persona, or share any of your values that are most firmly held. Share with your spouse these songs, along with a description of how music appeals to you? Why do you choose to share with them?

Swap Books

Swapping the recommended book with a partner is another personal (and probably scary) thing. What you like in reading can express some significant signals to your spouse about your personality are and what the things you appreciate. This exercise will show everything about them which have not been learned before, no matter how well you know your spouse. Reading a favorite novel is like having a glimpse into the mind of your partner. Diving through something in some of their most challenging years that had a significant effect on your partner is a great way to build a deep and intimate bond.

Conclusion

We are aware that communication is the transition from one location to another of knowledge. In relationships, contact helps you to clarify what you are feeling and what your desires are about someone else. Not only does the process of communication help to fulfill your desires, but it also encourages you to remain linked in your relationship. When you have thoughts or encounter stuff in the outside world, emotions are a given. You then bring words together to articulate your feelings and explain what you desire, believe, need, etc. Much of this exists at a subconscious stage, without the need to deliberate over anything you say. The difference exists when describing their internal or emotional feelings; various individuals use different phrases and vocabulary. If you use particular terms and phrases to explain things to another person, certain words and phrases can differ from how they might define the same event themselves. That ensures no one else will encounter or process the vocabulary you use entirely in precisely the same way as you do. Apply to this the reality that no one feels as you do precisely. We also had diverse views, and we viewed the universe differently and our position in it. All have various views and ideals that vary. Your interaction is focused on things that have occurred, things that are occurring, or things in existence that you like to happen. Mental thinking is still present, and it is something that differs from person to person. Imagine that as you are heading down the lane, a car pulls out in front of you. The mind processes the event until you inform the passenger something by considering: your beliefs, everything you deem essential in life. What you think people can and shouldn't do while driving and how people can and shouldn't handle each other are your convictions. Your past driving encounters and related circumstances. Your hopes and desires or worrying about what in the case might have happened. There are a lot of potential remarks you may make to your passenger in response after experiencing all of this on a subconscious level. Mentally map yourself back through the first months of dating your new spouse or girlfriend or boyfriend until you learn on. Please take a moment to remember how fun and intoxicating it feels to launch this relationship. It's been an exhilarating moment, has it? You were intensely infatuated, even in love already, and it all seemed so simple and perfect. You were totally conscious at the moment while you were with your girlfriend or boyfriend. It seems like everything about you was disappearing into the past when you just had eyes for each other. You find each other so insanely compelling and attractive that you would shift the heavens and the world as much as possible to be together. Your partner could do no wrong, and you were motivated to bring your best foot forward, with all your blazing beauty, to show your shiniest self. Also, your unexpected eagerness to shed the additional ten pounds to stay in shape could have shocked you. Talk to each other. You cannot interpret the mind of your partner, no matter how much you meet and respect each other. To prevent misunderstandings that may trigger damage, frustration, disappointment, or uncertainty, we need to communicate explicitly. It requires two people to have a relationship, and each individual has various requirements and modes of communicating. Couples ought to find a way that fits their relationship to connect. Safe forms of communication include preparation and rigorous work. It is possible to practice Clear and transparent communication. Some people find it daunting to articulate and will require patience and support to share their thoughts. These individuals may be effective listeners, or they may be individuals whose acts talk louder than their voices. Codependency comes in every shape and every size and with various intensity levels. It is fundamentally attributed to weak self-concept and bad limits, like an unwillingness to provide an opinion or say no. In all kinds of relationships, codependency may create, such as parent-child, relationship-partner, wife or husband-spouse, and even work colleague-boss. It's shockingly clear what will make a relationship work. Successful couples are no more educated, wealthier, or spiritually astute than most. Yet they have stumbled upon a dynamic in their day-to-day lives that prevents their pessimistic thoughts and emotions towards each other from overcoming their optimistic ones (which all couples have). They support each other's interests rather than building an atmosphere of disagreement and opposition. Conflict in a relationship may be a major cause of tension. If the tension in your relationship is unresolved, it causes uncertainty that will adversely impact both you and your partner's well-being and well-being. Here are a couple of ways you can be physically and emotionally impaired by disagreements in a relationship, along with several suggestions about how to handle this and cope. End of the day, this is life, and stuff happens to us. We have to go through highs and lows, anger and joy, conflicts, and compassion, but as long as we have each other with the right intention and an approach to taking every relationship in our life with sincerity, patience, and mindfulness, we are going to be okay.

CPSIA information can be obtained
at www.ICGtesting.com
Printed in the USA
LVHW040403151220
674158LV00028B/1492